TOWARDS COHESION POLICY 4.0

STRUCTURAL TRANSFORMATION AND INCLUSIVE GROWTH

John Bachtler, Joaquim Oliveira Martins, Peter Wostner and Piotr Zuber

OECD
BETTER POLICIES FOR BETTER LIVES

RSA Regional Studies Association
A leading & impactful community

RSA Europe, Brussels
Regional Studies Association

First published 2019
by Taylor & Francis
4 Park Square, Milton Park, Abingdon, Oxon, OX14 4RN

Taylor & Francis Group, an informa business

© 2019 John Bachtler, Joaquim Oliveira Martins,
Peter Wostner and Piotr Zuber

ISBN13: 978-0-367-24367-8 (print)
ISBN13: 978-0-429-28205-8 (e-book)

Typeset in 10.5/13.5 Univers LT Std
by Nova Techset Private Limited, Bengaluru and Chennai, India

Disclaimer

Every effort has been made to contact copyright holders for their permission to reprint material in this book. The publishers would be grateful to hear from any copyright holder who is not here acknowledged and will undertake to rectify any errors or omissions in future editions of this book.

CONTENTS

Preface   v
Authors   vii

Executive Summary   1

1. Introduction   3
    1.1 Political polarisation and inequality   4
    1.2 New opportunities and challenges   6
    1.3 Future EU policies for structural transformation and cohesion   7

2. **The Challenge of Economic Change for Europe**   9
    2.1 Global transformations – the fourth production revolution   10
    2.2 An opportunity for renewal   12
    2.3 Structural transformation and the importance of ecosystems   14

3. Structural Transformation and Productivity Challenges for the EU   17
    3.1 Why productivity is not resuming and how this affects inequality   18
    3.2 How regional disparities may affect EU productivity   21
    3.3 Differentiated regional productivity catching-up within
         EU countries   24

4. Territorial Policy Responses   29
    4.1 Strategies for global frontier regions   30
    4.2 Strategies for intermediate regions   31
    4.3 Strategies for lagging regions   32
    4.4 The case for an integrated system approach for regions and cities   34

5. **Developing a European Policy Response**   35
    5.1 Lessons from Lisbon and Europe 2020: Principles for a new
         EU strategy   36
    5.2 Focus and coherence: Improving the effectiveness of direct
         EU spending   38

6. **Ensuring Territorial and Socially Inclusive Growth: A More Effective Cohesion Policy**   43
    6.1 Strengthening the effectiveness of Cohesion Policy   44
    6.2 The efficiency of Cohesion Policy implementation   47
    6.3 Economic governance, EU sustainable growth and structural transformation strategy   49

7. **Conclusions and Recommendations**   53
    7.1 A new agenda for structural transformation and cohesion   54
    7.2 Recommendations   55

8. Bibliography   59
Annex 1: Regional Productivity Catching-Up in Selected EU Member States, 2000–2013   71

PREFACE

In the context of the current debate on the future of the EU and its Multiannual Financial Framework for 2021–2027, and specifically the role of EU Cohesion Policy, this book reflects on the opportunities and challenges of structural transformation in Europe and sets out proposals for policy change. It draws on the latest research from international bodies and academia, as well as new statistical analysis by the OECD on the performance of EU regions with respect to productivity. The book is also based on informal discussions and feedback from senior officials in several Member States, particularly concerning the reform of European economic governance, the relationship between EU policies under direct management and shared management, and the reform of Cohesion Policy. Lastly, the book takes account of critical comments on an earlier version of the book, published as a monograph in May 2017.

The authors are very grateful for the informal feedback from academic experts and senior officials received on earlier versions of the book. They also acknowledge the assistance of: Eric Gonnard and Alexander Lembcke of the OECD Regional Development Policy Division; research support from Dr Carlos Mendez, Dr Laura Polverari and Dr Neculai-Cristian Surubaru of the European Policies Research Centre (University of Strathclyde); critical comment on the structural transformation agenda from Professor David Bailey (Department of Economics, Finance & Entrepreneurship, Aston University); and administrative support from Alyson Ross and Dr Keith Clement. Lastly, the authors would like to thank the Regional Studies Association and RSA Europe for publishing the book.

August 2018

AUTHORS

The book has been written by **Professor John Bachtler** (Director, European Policies Research Centre, University of Strathclyde, United Kingdom), **Dr Joaquim Oliveira Martins** (Special Advisor to the Director, Centre for Entrepreneurship, SMEs, Regions and Cities, Organisation for Economic Cooperation and Development), **Dr Peter Wostner** (Expert working at the Government Office for Structural Policy, Slovenia) and **Dr Piotr Zuber** (Faculty of Geography and Regional Studies, University of Warsaw, and Adviser and former Director of the Department of Structural Policy Coordination, Ministry of Economic Development, Poland).

It should be noted that the authors are writing in a personal capacity, and the views expressed do not necessarily reflect the views of the OECD (or its Member States) or the governments of Poland and Slovenia.

EXECUTIVE SUMMARY

As the debate on the direction of the EU and the Multiannual Financial Framework for 2021–2027 intensifies, there are important questions about how the EU can best deploy its budgetary resources to meet the challenges facing the Union. The current precarious state of European integration and its uncertain future were clearly set out in the 2017 White Paper on the Future of Europe and reiterated in a range of academic and policy research. The continuing effects of the financial, economic and migration crises are associated with reduced confidence and trust in democratic institutions and politicians, and a rise in populism, threatening the unity of the EU.

A major cause is the unequal impact of globalisation and technological change on different parts of the EU. This book argues that the EU not only needs to accelerate sustainable growth but also to resume convergence so that all parts of the EU are able to exploit the opportunities from the globalisation of trade and technological change.

The current economic situation in the EU is characterised by persistently low labour productivity growth at below one percent per year. Research suggests that the main source of the productivity slowdown is not a lower rate of innovation by the most advanced firms, sectors or regions, but rather a slowing of the pace at which innovations spread throughout the economy. At regional level, there is an increasing productivity gap between leading 'frontier' regions and lagging regions, a gap that grew by 56 percent between 1995 and 2014. This is part of a broader trend of growing distance between the leading regions and most other regions. The inequalities across EU countries are now accounted for substantially by differences *within* rather than *between* countries.

Renewing the successful European economic growth model depends on the EU's ability to reduce the regional productivity gap, in particular, the rate at which the diffusion of innovation and structural change takes place. There is significant untapped potential to increase nationwide productivity by improving the performance of regions.

If EU and Member State policymakers are to exploit fully the opportunities of the fourth industrial revolution, they need to develop or adapt policy frameworks and strategies that will stimulate inclusive and sustainable growth, especially access to employment and capacity for entrepreneurship. This demands a more granular approach to structural policy, tailored better to the specific conditions of the different types of regions and communities across the EU. Different strategies are needed for frontier regions, intermediate regions (some 'catching up' but others only 'keeping pace') and lagging regions.

Existing EU strategies – from Lisbon/Gothenburg to Europe 2020 – have been only partially successful, with limited results in relation to the scale of the challenge. In particular, policy responses have given

https://doi.org/10.1080/2578711X.2019.1547481

inadequate recognition to the spatial unevenness of development opportunities and challenges for economic growth and development in the EU. With relatively limited budgetary resources at EU level, a new EU strategy is needed based on the following four principles:

Four principles for new EU strategy

- a limited number of key priorities that collectively promote accelerated innovation, structural transformation and inclusive and environmentally sustainable growth;
- more effective and efficient governance to ensure institutional coordination, and integration horizontally across the policy domains at EU, Member State and regional levels, and vertically between EU, national and regional levels;
- structural reforms and investment in institutional capacity to optimise the conditions for reform and investment, particularly in the regulation of labour markets and other areas; and
- territorial and social inclusion, by taking account of territorial differences in the formulation and implementation of policies.

The critical requirement is a coherent, consistent and mutually reinforcing policy framework. Sectoral policies cannot deliver on a new EU agenda without integrated territorial policy packages. Equally, integrated territorial policy approaches cannot deliver prosperity and inclusive growth in the regions without well-designed sectoral and structural policies and reforms.

The post-2020 reform of EU policies, therefore, needs a new strategy for sustainable growth and structural transformation, setting out a common policy vision and a coherent framework for all EU policies – through regulatory reform, directly managed and territorial policies – with a collective focus on improving the ecosystems for structural change at different levels.

This needs a commitment by governments at different levels to work together to facilitate concerted and integrated action, combining a mix of policy inputs, to meet different territorial development needs and challenges. Part of the agenda should involve a reformed economic governance system to provide an integrated framework for economic policy coordination, as well as a mix of incentives and conditionalities to ensure that structural reforms are carried out. A new EU strategy also needs to be underpinned by a performance and accountability framework covering all areas of EU spending.

Within this integrated approach to cohesive and inclusive growth, EU Cohesion Policy plays a crucial role in ensuring territorially differentiated policy support to promote structural transformation through innovation-oriented ecosystems at regional and local levels.

The priority for Cohesion Policy in 2021–27 is to maintain the key principles of the 2013 regulatory reform. However, changes are needed to maximise opportunities to influence structural transformation, including: better coordination of funding instruments; recognition of the different territorial opportunities and challenges for frontier, intermediate and lagging regions; more emphasis on human capital; strengthened conditionalities; investment in capacity-building; and a significantly rationalised and differentiated implementation system.

https://doi.org/10.1080/2578711X.2019.1547481

1. INTRODUCTION

In 2017, the White Paper on the Future of Europe made a powerful statement about the current precarious state of European integration and its uncertain future. The continuing effects of the financial, economic and migration crises are associated with reduced confidence and trust in democratic institutions and politicians, as well as a rise in populism, threatening the unity of the EU. As the European Commission recognised in subsequent 'reflections papers' and (to a certain extent) its proposals for the EU budget in 2021–2027, the fundamental cause is the highly unequal impact of globalisation and technological change on different parts of the EU. Many regions have been able to exploit the opportunities of structural change, but equally there are regions and social groups that have been left behind. The challenge for the EU is not only to accelerate growth but also to resume convergence to ensure that all parts of the EU are able to exploit the growing globalisation of trade and technological change. Growth needs to be sustainable, cohesive and inclusive: it should deliver prosperity for the whole of Europe.

In the context of the debate on the future of the EU, and specifically the EU policy and budgetary priorities after 2020, this book makes the case for a new approach to structural transformation, growth and cohesion in the EU. Drawing on recent research by international bodies (EC, OECD and World Bank) and from academic studies, the book explores the opportunities and challenges from globalisation and technological change, the widening differences in productivity between leading and lagging regions, and the need for a new EU policy framework capable of delivering inclusive growth.

1.1 POLITICAL POLARISATION AND INEQUALITY

According to Eurobarometer data for the past decade, the trust of citizens in the EU is only slowly recovering; the 2018 data indicate that only 42 percent of EU citizens have trust in the EU, an increase on the low point of 31 percent between 2012 and 2014, but still well below the high point of 57 percent in 2007 (European Commission 2016a, 2018a). Further, the EU28 figure encompasses a wide range of opinion at Member State level, with very low levels of trust in Greece (27 percent), France (34 percent), Italy (36 percent) and Czech Republic (37 percent) – all of which were countries where trust in the EU was between 50 and 65 percent in the early 2000s (European Commission 2005a, 2016a). There has also been an unprecedented upsurge in support for Eurosceptic parties across the EU, most clearly in the 2014 European Parliament elections (Treib 2014) and deep territorial divisions in voting patterns in elections and referenda over the past five years.

While the factors at play are complex and contested, it is clear that the eurozone and migration crises have politicised the EU in public debates, diminished confidence in EU institutions and boosted support for Eurosceptic political parties (Hobolt and de Vries 2016; Hobolt and Tilley 2016; Hooghe and Marks 2017). The key factors explaining defection from mainstream pro-European to Eurosceptic parties are the degree to which individuals were negatively affected by the crisis and their discontent with the EU's response to the crisis (Hobolt and de Vries 2016). Identity politics associated with community, cohesion and solidarity have been at the core of Eurosceptic party narratives and electoral gains (Börzel and Risse 2017). The principle of EU solidarity across Member States has been challenged by the euro crisis and the politics surrounding

https://doi.org/10.1080/2578711X.2019.1547482

bailouts, while the migration/refugee crisis has led to reactions against the core principle of freedom of movement and the liberal foundations of the European project in favour of exclusionary and nationalist agendas.

An important factor is perceptions of an unequal Europe. Eurobarometer survey research indicates that just over half of citizens surveyed do not agree that everyone in their country has a chance to succeed in life. In the view of citizens, social equality, solidarity and comparable living standards across the EU are regarded as most important for the future of the EU (European Commission 2016a, 2016d). Various studies have shown that economic factors impact on political support for the EU. Poor economic performance at the national level (in terms of GDP/GNI and unemployment change) or negative subjective perceptions among citizens about globalisation and their economic future reduce political support for the EU (Hooghe and Marks 2004; Henjak et al. 2012; Chalmers and Dellmuth 2015; Lastra-Anadón and Muñiz 2017) and encourage support for more radical parties on both the right and the left (Beaudonnet and Gomez 2016; Rooduijn et al. 2017).

Initial research on the patterns of voting behaviour in the United Kingdom's EU referendum in June 2016 found that inequality, associated with the negative effects of integration and globalisation, was one explanatory factor; those areas with lower median wages, low levels of skills, lack of opportunities and higher levels of poverty were significantly more likely to vote Leave (Bell and Machin 2016; Darvas and Wolff 2016; Goodwin and Heath 2016; Clarke et al. 2017). This is part of a broader pattern, as Rodríguez-Pose (2017: 189) argues:

Persistent poverty, economic decay and lack of opportunities are at the root of considerable discontent in declining and lagging-behind areas the world over. Poor development prospects and an increasing belief that these places have 'no future' – as economic dynamism has been posited to be increasingly dependent on agglomeration economies – have led many of these so-called 'places that don't matter' to revolt against the status quo.

Evidence from EU countries shows that fears about globalisation influences are greatest among less educated, less affluent and older people, who have a greater propensity to support populist and anti-EU parties (De Vries and Hoffman 2016). Income inequality in the EU has also been found to undermine support for democracy and trust in politicians and parliaments (Schäfer 2012). A recent study, using European Election Study data from 2009, shows that citizens who have greater levels of concern about inequality and favour more redistribution tend to have lower political support for the EU as it is now, but are relatively more favourable to further European integration (Simpson and Loveless 2016).

EU policymakers increasingly recognise that growth and integration have failed to give sufficient attention to solidarity and cohesion (Buti and Pichelman 2017):

While the deepening globalisation and integration process has generated overall income gain … [it has created] … winners (take it all) and losers in an age of massive transformation … In this context, EU institutional settings and policies have been increasingly perceived as pro-market biased, paying little attention if any to its social impact, and undermining cohesion, solidarity, autonomy and governability at the national, regional and local level.

1.2 NEW OPPORTUNITIES AND CHALLENGES

The question facing the EU is how to respond. The long-term convergence of structurally weaker countries and regions with the rest of the EU was exacerbated by the financial and economic crises, with rising disparities within and between countries (European Commission 2014a). All Member States were affected by the crisis, but with strong national and regional variations in the scale and timing of impact, and in the pace and degree of recovery (Crescenzi et al. 2016a). In 11 EU Member States, GDP in 2015 remained lower than in 2007 (at constant prices). Most EU countries have seen positive economic growth since at least 2014, and for the first time since the crisis, all EU economies expanded in 2017 – but rates of growth and job creation remain muted in some countries (European Commission 2016c, 2018b). Among the less-developed regions, different patterns can be discerned between low-growth and low-income regions, linked to different trajectories of regional economic restructuring and the quality of governance (European Commission 2017a). Low-income regions improved their productivity and growth even during the crisis, while low-growth regions did not become more productive and lost pre-2008 employment gains. Macroeconomic imbalances played a role in this latter group in exacerbating the effects of the crisis.

Further, there is the prospect of massive structural transformation over the coming decades that will create major new opportunities for the EU but also huge challenges in providing EU citizens with secure and well-paid employment. Different parts of the EU are better placed than others to respond: the productivity gap between the frontier regions and the lagging regions is widening.

Policy responses need to recognise that current and future opportunities and challenges for economic growth and development in the EU are spatially highly uneven. The ability of the EU to exploit opportunities and overcome challenges is place-specific, contingent on factors such as historical legacies, resources and institutions (Iammarino et al. 2017). Regional and other spatial policies are sometimes judged less optimal than spatially blind policy responses. Yet, no policy is spatially neutral or blind; any form of government intervention has spatial consequences, and many sectoral policies implicitly or explicitly favour growth in certain areas.

The EU's main instrument for responding to uneven development is Cohesion Policy, which has an increasingly strong track record of performance. During the 1990s, critics rightly highlighted ineffective EU spending, typified by examples of investment in underused infrastructure. Such criticisms were valid in the 1990s, but successive reforms during the 2000s (most notably in 2013) have mobilised a major shift in Cohesion Policy spending towards Europe 2020 priorities and a focus on performance, with increasingly convincing research evidence on the effectiveness of the policy (Bachtler et al. 2017; Davies 2017). During the economic crisis, the policy also demonstrated its value as a stabilising and spatially targeted response to economic shocks; it sustained public investment in the face of enforced national austerity policies and fiscal retrenchment (McGregor et al. 2014).

The White Paper on the Future of Europe set out different budgetary and policy options for the future of Cohesion Policy: sustain and enhance (increased budget and new momentum); maintain and support (less funding but little change); prioritise and improve (focused support and spatial coverage); refresh and restart (radical change in direction and architecture); and reduction of priorities (sectoral refocus). Of these, the proposals put forward by the European Commission in May 2018 is closest to 'maintain and support' with less funding specifically for Cohesion Policy within the 'Cohesion and Values' heading and more thematic concentration – especially innovation and conditionalities (European Commission 2018c).

As the negotiations within the Council and European Parliament progress, this book makes the case for a substantial 'refresh' and 'enhancement' of the EU's approach to Cohesion Policy but set within a broader EU strategy towards growth and cohesion that responds to the opportunities and challenges of structural transformation – in effect, a 'Cohesion Policy 4.0'.[1] If EU integration is to deliver opportunity and prosperity to all EU citizens, including those left behind in the so-called developed regions of the EU, it needs to re-assess how it meets its Treaty objectives of economic, social and territorial cohesion. This needs to be considered in the wider context of structural transformation. Due to the next production revolution, the EU will need to restructure its policy approach. Member States and EU institutions need to work together to integrate both growth and cohesion objectives into EU, national, regional and local policies in a consistent, efficient and targeted fashion.

1.3 FUTURE EU POLICIES FOR STRUCTURAL TRANSFORMATION AND COHESION

The next chapters begin by outlining the challenge of economic change for Europe, in terms of both the implications of continuing globalisation and technological change and the opportunities for the EU from the renewal of economic competitiveness (Chapter 2) – requiring important changes to the current policy and institutional approach.

The book argues that renewing the successful European economic growth model depends on its ability to reduce the increasing productivity gap between 'frontier regions' and other parts of the EU, in particular, the rate at which the diffusion of innovation and structural change takes place (Chapter 3). Importantly, inequalities in economic growth and development across the EU are now accounted for by differences *within* rather than *between* countries. With many frontier regions being capital cities or other major urban areas, there is a real danger of increasing economic and social disconnection between the flourishing 'motors' of EU growth and the remainder of the EU. That said, frontier regions are also faced with a number of challenges, some of which should also be addressed within the EU policy framework.

The challenge for EU and Member State policymakers is to develop or adapt policy frameworks and strategies that will stimulate growth, but in a manner, that also ensures greater inclusiveness (Chapter 4), especially in access to employment opportunities and capacity for entrepreneurship. This demands a more granular approach to structural policy, which is better tailored to the specific conditions of the different types of cities and regions across the EU and with greater consideration of governance requirements.

---

[1] The proposals in this book foresee a 'fourth generation Cohesion Policy' that follows on from the first generation (1975–1988), second generation (1988–2006) and third generation (2007–2020).

https://doi.org/10.1080/2578711X.2019.1547482

The starting point for a European policy response is that existing strategies – from Lisbon/Gothenburg to Europe 2020 – have been only partially successful, with limited results in relation to the scale of the challenge (Chapter 5). Notwithstanding certain achievements, strategies have been over-ambitious in relation to the resources available, the deficits in governance (especially on coherence and the coordination of policies) and the performance of interventions. On the one hand, those policy levers that are directly managed by the EU are insufficiently discriminating towards the different development situations and institutional contexts in different parts of the EU; and in some cases there remain important questions about their additionality and effectiveness. On the other hand, the main EU policy that is regionally discriminatory – Cohesion Policy – is demonstrating evidence of increasing effectiveness, but its performance is constrained by the quality of government, especially the need for structural reforms and deficits in institutional and administrative capacity (Charron et al. 2014; Surubaru 2017). Both sets of EU policies need better coordination with Member State policies with a more effective system of economic governance (Chapter 6).

Looking forward, if the EU is to exploit the potential of the new production revolution in ways that benefit all EU citizens, it needs a structural transformation agenda that recognises more consistently – across all relevant policies – the different potentials of regions in Europe and includes a commitment to sustainable, inclusive and cohesive growth (Chapter 7).

https://doi.org/10.1080/2578711X.2019.1547482

2. THE CHALLENGE OF ECONOMIC CHANGE FOR EUROPE

2.1 GLOBAL TRANSFORMATIONS – THE FOURTH PRODUCTION REVOLUTION

The past three decades have been characterised by trade liberalisation, the rise of global value chains (Gereffi and Fernandes-Stark 2011) and global production networks (Coe and Yeung 2015; Dicken 2014). Emerging countries from across the globe have been integrated into the world economy (OECD 2013a), shifting the centre of global economic gravity towards Southeast Asia (Kharas 2010; Quah 2011; Toth and Nagy 2016). Labour cost advantages, in particular, attracted investment and process-oriented production to emerging countries, stimulating unprecedented growth especially in China and India. The cumulative causation of rapidly growing market demand coupled with large populations generated a strong pull effect, in turn attracting additional production activities (OECD 2013a).

This process has allowed some emerging economies gradually to increase the sophistication of their export base (Schott 2008; IMF 2011) and to move from parts-assemblers to parts-providers (OECD 2013a). It is increasingly evident that the more advanced emerging economies are also becoming significant players in the knowledge-intensive segments of production processes, triggering concerns in the developed world about the consequences for their economies, especially with respect to future employment.

China has been the major focus. Its share of high-quality and high-price exports increased significantly; between 2005 and 2011, full-package manufacturing as a share of total export trade rose from 42 to 70 percent. China is already a runner-up after the US in terms of investment in R&D, and its share of world exports in commercial knowledge-intensive services has reached 10 percent (OECD 2013c). More broadly, it has been estimated that Asia's share (excluding Japan) of the world middle class could rise from 10 percent in 2000 to 40 percent by 2040 (Kharas 2010), with a billion new middle-class consumers forecast to emerge in 12 Asian countries over the next decade (Ogilvy and Mather 2016).

These trends are frequently represented as a major threat for the developed world and the EU's attractiveness as a production location, because of fears of import competition and off-shoring of the production of goods and services. In academic and policy research, China's import penetration, especially after its entry into the WTO in 2001, is associated with employment losses in manufacturing and routine jobs in the developed economies, both in the US (Autor et al. 2013) and in Europe (Balsvik et al. 2013; Donoso et al. 2014; Dauth et al. 2014; Keller and Utar 2016; Breemersch et al. 2016).

A further dimension of perceived risks is technological change and digital transformation due to automation processes in particular. Indeed, the latter has been termed the fourth production revolution (De Propris/WEF 2016). Research has highlighted two important implications. First, technological change is said potentially to involve jobless growth, making unemployment and underemployment the most important business risks globally (De Propris/WEF 2016). It has been estimated that 'as many as 45 percent of the activities individuals are paid to perform' are open to automation according to McKinsey (Chui et al. 2015). This conclusion is supported by other studies (Frey and Osborne 2013; PwC 2017), though not all have such

https://doi.org/10.1080/2578711X.2019.1547484

dramatic conclusions (e.g. Arntz et al. 2016).[2] Future automation will not only affect routine and codifiable activities, but also those that require tacit knowledge and experience, i.e. those parts of activities where developed countries have a comparative advantage (Rifkin 2014). According to the OECD (2015a), 'about 60 per cent of occupations could have 30 per cent or more of their constituent activities automated'. This would dramatically transform the vast majority of occupations, possibly leading either to jobless growth and/or a further strengthening of job polarisation in the labour markets of developed economies (OECD 2015a), potentially further aggravating political polarisation.

The likely impact of these scenarios is still speculative. Analysis by OECD (2015b) found no evidence that the application of ICT has increased technological unemployment overall, while Breemersch et al. (2016) found that changes in employment (both in manufacturing and non-manufacturing industries) were only weakly correlated with technological change in the case of 18 European countries between 1996 and 2007. Importantly, the employment gains and losses from technological change vary considerably across the labour market. Technological change through adoption of ICT and R&D and related process innovation are associated with polarisation of high-paid jobs within individual manufacturing industries (Breemersch et al. 2016). There is also evidence of technology affecting the polarisation of low-paid employment in Western and Northern European countries (ibid. 29).

The second, complementary, perceived threat is specific to Europe: concerns that the EU is falling behind technologically, with potentially devastating welfare effects on the European Social Model, especially with 'winner-takes-all' types of markets becoming more important, i.e. markets where market leaders capture significant and increasing market shares (Andrews et al. 2016). Although Europe generally has a strong position with respect to advances in technology, value-added, productivity, profitability and profits, there are important questions about its technological leadership.

The EU continues to lag behind the US in terms of innovation performance. On the input side, R&D spending has stagnated at two percent of GDP since 2000, far below the target rate of three percent called for under the Lisbon and then Europe 2020 strategies, and below the 2.8 percent recorded in the US (Aiginger 2016). Meanwhile, China is steadily advancing towards the European R&D intensity level (ibid.). Further, frequently discussed EU-US gaps relate to university rankings and venture capital financing of start-ups. At the level of outcomes or industrial performance, a key EU deficit versus the US consists of the lack of so-called 'yollies', or young leading innovators in knowledge-intensive sectors that grow to become large, R&D-intensive firms (Veugelers and Cincera 2010; Cincera and Veugelers 2014). There are few firms in the EU that can be compared with Apple, Google, Facebook or Tesla. Indeed, in the ICT field, there is no European company among the global top 20 companies (Roland Berger 2015). The OECD (2017a) found that the EU is lagging behind countries like the US, Japan, and even Korea and China, with regard to the share of value-added in ICT goods and services in total manufacturing exports, the share of ICT-related

---

[2] Frey and Osborne's (2013) work was re-examined by Arntz et al. (2016). Using a new OECD dataset, they suggested that ten percent of jobs were subject to 'high risk' (i.e. 70 percent probability) of computerisation.

patents in total patents, or in ICT investment as a share of GDP.[3] The rising role of the (technology) platform economy further underlines the importance of achieving substantial European participation in this new 'mega-trend' (OECD 2016a).

ICT is not the only example of insufficient European leadership in the technology field. While Europe is clearly maintaining a competitive global position in a number of high value-added products – especially in higher-technology sectors – there is a widening gap of industrial dynamics within Europe, with a lack of investment in industrial modernisation, and the age of installed process technology in Europe is increasing rather than decreasing (Kroll et al. 2016). Further, the obsolescence of production facilities seems to be concentrated in certain EU Member States, such as France and the United Kingdom, compared to Germany or Sweden (SYMOP et al. 2014; Kroll et al. 2016). The decline in innovative performance has also been recognised as an important issue at the regional level (European Commission 2016b), explored further in the subsequent chapters of this book.

2.2 AN OPPORTUNITY FOR RENEWAL

While the challenges of globalisation and technological change are often presented as daunting, it is important to stress that there are major opportunities which the EU is well-placed to exploit – if the EU is able to respond adequately to the challenges. Indeed, the OECD considers that the next production revolution has the potential 'to restore the competitiveness' of developed economies (OECD 2017b). It argues that this is where the future policy focus should be directed: embracing global transformations as an opportunity to empower people, regions and communities to engage with and influence change.

The first factor creating a more favourable global context is the erosion of the cost advantages of at least some of the major emerging economies. According to the Boston Consulting Group (2014), the manufacturing costs of countries like China and Thailand are already almost on a par with Poland and the Czech Republic and only some 20 percent behind Germany or Sweden. In countries such as China, average hourly wage increases of 15–20 percent in recent years (while being a benefit of globalisation for Chinese workers) have eroded the country's cost advantage in labour-intensive activities (OECD 2013a, 2013b).

While there are many other emerging economies in Asia and Africa that still have low-cost advantages and are trying to replicate the Chinese model, it is still the case that the pressure on the developed economies will not be as acute as in the last 15 years. The reduced off-shoring pressure is likely to be further reduced due to the discovery of hidden costs (Porter and Rivkin 2012), rising uncertainties and the need to ensure supply chain resilience (e.g. in managing the effects of conflicts or natural disasters). This is combined with the realisation by multinationals that interrupted/ disrupted production chains are costly, especially

---

[3] France represents a positive exception as far as ICT investment is concerned, as it is almost on a par with Japan and the US, with around three percent of ICT-related investments in its GDP, and even exhibited an increasing investment trend between 2004 and 2014. Germany, on the other hand, is still lagging behind significantly at below two percent and with a downward trend (OECD 2017a).

https://doi.org/10.1080/2578711X.2019.1547484

with the growing need for operational flexibility, efficient cooperation and coordination across different production stages, and the desire to ensure quality and reduce lead times so as to respond more flexibly to demand (OECD 2013a; De Backer et al. 2016; Bailey and De Propris 2014). In addition, the declining share of labour in overall costs means that labour costs are a less critical factor in location decisions as a consequence of the automation processes of the fourth industrial revolution (OECD 2013b, 2013c).

These projected trends do not guarantee the renewed competitiveness of developed economies, for which the evidence is limited and mixed. There is, for example, no consensus on the importance of relocating production back to development economies (De Backer et al. 2016; Bailey and De Propris 2014). However, evidence does suggest that companies are faced with a changing cost calculus with regard to the optimal location of production, and companies will need to engage in different processes, collectively termed 'reshoring' (McKinsey & Co. 2014; Bailey and De Propris 2014).[4] Ellram et al. (2013) argue that firms are no longer looking at location costs 'in isolation' but are instead looking at total costs. Gray et al. (2013) also support the idea that reshoring is fundamentally about location. They note that firms' outsourcing probably took place faster than expected, as firms followed a herd instinct (a 'bandwagon effect') and internationalised their production, which, in some cases, led them to miscalculate the actual cost advantage of offshoring.

OECD work on future scenarios of production and trade within global value chains by 2030 concluded that 'rising wage costs in (some) emerging economies and the growing digitalisation of production … are expected to restore the competitiveness of developed economies and discourage further offshoring to emerging economies' (OECD 2017b: 2). They characterise the digitalisation of production to be 'the biggest game-changer, reversing the importance and length of GVCs [global value chains] and reorienting global production and trade back towards OECD economies' (ibid.).

A critical factor determining whether and to what extent a rebalancing takes place in the fourth production revolution is the ability of the developed economies to effect the necessary structural transformation (OECD 2017d). The key characteristics of future 'Industry 4.0' production are complex, rapidly responsive, creative, customised, digital, smart and intelligent, sustainable systems of production, with goods and services bundled together (OECD 2015c; De Propris/WEF 2016). Critically, production is also expected to become more distributed and localised, i.e. to get closer to the end markets (ibid.), which clearly represents a major opportunity not just for the core areas of the EU, but for regions and communities across the EU.

Making Europe attractive as a production and investment site for these forms of production, and thereby accelerating growth, will require profound and broad engagement by policymakers, business and wider society. Roland Berger (2014: 44) estimated that European economies were 'poised to embark on a radical structural transition' that over a 15-year period would require a total investment of €1,350 billion, on the basis of which Europe could see its manufacturing industry add gross value worth €1.25 trillion. Equally,

---

[4] The current literature presents a number of concepts, ranging from 'back-shoring' (suggesting the reverse of a previously offshored activity) to 'near-shoring' (suggesting an increased spatial proximity of value-chain activities, but not necessarily moved back to the home economy), or more generally 'best-shoring' (suggesting changes in the location of foreign activities) (Colliers International and Corenet Global 2013).

https://doi.org/10.1080/2578711X.2019.1547484

it is estimated that, without sufficient structural transformation, Europe could suffer a loss of €605 billion in foregone value-added.

This growth will not necessarily be inclusive with regard to employment. Research suggests that the employment impact may be limited due to automation (De Backer et al. 2016; OECD 2017b; Bailey and De Propris 2014). Productivity growth and new technologies will create new and complementary jobs (Autor 2015; Moretti 2010; Goos et al. 2015) but require significant and wide-ranging upskilling (OECD 2017a) and other investment in knowledge-based capital (OECD 2015d; Aiginger 2016). Consequently, the extent to which future growth is also inclusive depends on Europe's ability to facilitate a faster, more comprehensive, integrated and consistent approach to structural transformation than it has yet achieved. The next section explores in more detail why a comprehensive, multi-sectoral, multi-policy and even multi-disciplinary and cross-territorial (integrated) approach is essential for structural transformation.

2.3 STRUCTURAL TRANSFORMATION AND THE IMPORTANCE OF ECOSYSTEMS

The scale, scope and speed of the challenge of structural transformation indicate the requirement for a fundamentally different policy and institutional approach. Instead of the delivery of policies through (for example) aid schemes and projects, an increased focus will need to be placed on developing 'ecosystems' of open, interconnected networks of stakeholders, cooperating to a much greater extent through strategic partnerships. These will be much more dependent on their business environments to source ideas and solutions both locally (e.g. importance of knowledge-based factors such as links to universities or cooperation with technology parks) and globally (Roland Berger 2015; OECD 2015d; OECD 2017c; Wostner 2017; European Commission 2017a, 2017b).

There is no academic consensus on the differences between an innovation system and an innovation ecosystem, but the latter places particular emphasis on changes that (this book argues) should be at the forefront of future EU policy consideration. The innovation ecosystem approach focuses on both formal, scientific and informal, non-R&D-related innovation, and it stresses the importance of economic context (*milieu*), i.e. networks of sustainable linkages between individuals and organisations whose purpose includes the co-creation of value through collaboration (Smorodinskaya et al. 2017; Smorodinskaya and Katukov, 2017). Further the *eco*system approach distinguishes itself from the 'rigid hierarchical design of economic systems in the age of linear development' (ibid: 5248) and highlights 'the ability of collaborative networks to adapt themselves to a non-linear environment' featuring characteristics like agility, self-organisation, self-governance and synergy effects (ibid.). These, it is argued, seem to be much more conducive to the innovation-intensive, knowledge-based economies, which require organisational transformation into network-based production systems.

There are three sets of factors that specifically support the need for an 'ecosystem approach' to structural transformation. First, the unprecedented speed of technological, market and social changes translates into a highly uncertain environment for business and government. Combined with increasing complexities this means greater risks, especially given research-to-market time delays. Managing this uncertainty and risk

https://doi.org/10.1080/2578711X.2019.1547484

requires the pooling of resources and risk-sharing but also the need to work with joint infrastructures and support services, such as involvement in living labs where multinational as well as start-up companies can meet and benefit from each other's advantages (capital and networks for the former and innovative approaches and speed by the latter). Such support environments, which translate into globally connected (innovative) ecosystems, will unavoidably need to be tailored to specific national, regional or even local contexts.[5] Indeed, as shown by the European Commission (2017a, 2017b), it is not just that they need to be tailored, but they can only be provided at the regional and local levels, though integrated vertically in the broader policy mix at national and European levels.

A second major factor is that innovation and especially disruptive innovation and creativity require multi-disciplinarity and open models of collaboration (Chesbrough 2003). As argued by OECD (2016c: 68):

> [the] pieces of knowledge required come from various actors and activities are rarely available inside a single organisation … so it is important therefore to support the generation, diffusion and use of many sorts of knowledge and types of collaboration.

This not only requires convergence or 'mixing' of different technologies (OECD, 2015c) or industries, and the mixing of different skills where 'interdisciplinary thinking is key' (Roland Berger 2014: 12), but also combinations of the four modalities of human behaviour – science, engineering, design and arts (Oxman 2016). Such convergence or 'mixing' requires an open and collaborative atmosphere based on established relationships and trust, with the latter being needed even to explore the possibilities of collaboration (Wostner 2017). In turn, this requires well-developed institutions capable of nurturing collaboration and networks both regionally (territorially) and internationally (Amison and Bailey 2014) and in industrial policy terms to bring actors together in a process of knowledge discovery (Rodrik 2009, 2013).

Linked to the latter, a third factor is the importance of proximity to comprehensive and integrated support environments. It has been shown empirically that proximity, especially to the urban centres, matters for economic growth (Brakman and van Marrewijk 2007; OECD 2014). Proximity to large urban agglomerations seems to enable rural regions to borrow agglomeration effects from the urban areas, provided that a certain threshold of connectivity and linkages is ensured (Veneri and Ruiz 2013; Ahrend and Schumann 2014). Such urban-rural linkages can have important catching-up effects, given that 80 percent of the rural population within OECD countries live close to cities.

That said, linkages function *not only* on the regional level, they also operate at the local level (Duranton and Overman 2005). This applies particularly where there is a co-location of firms, researchers and workers,

---

[5] On innovation policy, for example, see Veugelers (2015) on 'innovation capacity' and catching up. She argues that this needs a systemic, long-term and dynamic policy mix that takes into account countries' initial strengths and weaknesses and supports the potential of the country for innovation-based development by: providing framework conditions; promoting access to (foreign) technologies; supporting the building of absorptive as well as creative capacities; and supporting links across innovation agents. Overall, this calls for high-quality institutions involved in the design and implementation of innovation policy (Badinger et al. 2016).

especially when combined with trust-based institutional structures and supported by policy, facilitating the generation and transfer of knowledge. In areas such as entrepreneurship, localisation economies decline rapidly over relatively short distances, and multidisciplinarity, new ideas and mixing of technology and skills, by and large, come from actual face-to-face interaction and developed social relations and institutions, further underlining the need for a territorial policy approach (Rosenthal and Strange 2003; Storper and Venables 2004; Feldman and Kogler 2010; Rekers and Hansen 2015).

The challenge for policymakers is that the promotion of environments conducive to innovation in line with the fourth production revolution thus requires the engagement of multiple policies, in a consistent and coordinated manner. It is essential that policy-mixes are not just adapted, but also integrated. As shown by Wostner (2017), for regions and countries to advance, a series of conditions need to be provided simultaneously, from RTDI (Research and Technical Development Infrastructure) and human resource development, to entrepreneurship and infrastructure provision, and they need to be provided in line with longer-term development priorities (as set out, for example, in the smart specialisation strategies), reflecting the comparative advantages and needs of particular territories (Crescenzi et al. 2016a). The same messages flow from the literature on advanced manufacturing (Kroll et al. 2016), digitalisation and the next production revolution (Roland Berger 2015; OECD 2017c), as well as on employment and inclusion from regional and local perspectives (OECD 2010, 2011, 2016a, 2016c, 2016e).

Further, the linkages between urban and rural areas mean that 'policy-mixing' should systematically encourage partnerships among people, firms and institutions across different territories in multi-sectoral, multi-policy and cross-territorial frameworks. The OECD has argued that policy packages to develop such ecosystems should be delivered through a combination of national, regional and local levels, while being adapted to the needs of different territories (OECD 2017c).

https://doi.org/10.1080/2578711X.2019.1547484

3. STRUCTURAL TRANSFORMATION AND PRODUCTIVITY CHALLENGES FOR THE EU

The current economic situation in the EU is characterised by persistently low labour productivity growth, at below one percent per year.[6] Other major OECD regions, such as Japan or the US, share the same pattern. This is a major concern for governments. In the long run, productivity is indeed the main driver of income growth, especially in economies affected by ageing and demographic decline.[7] Economic crises usually reignite productivity through a cleansing effect, which deleverages the economy towards high-productivity sectors. However, the effects of the 2008 crisis seem subdued in this respect.

Productivity growth is the key economic indicator of innovation, and it is only through increasing total factor productivity growth that a real increase in wellbeing, as well as the capacity to address other challenges, can be sustained (Jorgenson et al. 2014). That said, while productivity growth is the key factor deserving attention, GDP per capita growth rates have to be as high as the increase in labour productivity to stabilise employment (Aiginger 2016), which is also an EU policy priority (European Commission 2017c).

In consequence, governments are looking for new options to stimulate the growth of EU economies, but in a manner ensuring equity in access to opportunities, i.e. inclusion (Aiginger 2016; Badinger et al. 2016). This has generated the need to construct a broader development model involving a more granular approach to structural policy, which is able to mobilise the specific productivity drivers existing in different types of cities and regions.

3.1 WHY PRODUCTIVITY IS NOT RESUMING AND HOW THIS AFFECTS INEQUALITY

OECD research (2015e, 2016c) suggests that the main source of the productivity slowdown is not a lower rate of innovation by the most advanced firms, sectors or regions, but rather a slowing of the pace at which innovations spread throughout the economy. In other words, the 'diffusion machine' has broken down. This connects the question of territorial opportunities and cohesion with an aggregate *inclusive growth* agenda.

At the regional level, the OECD (2016c) has shown that the gap between the regions representing the 'frontier' of GDP per worker (a proxy for productivity levels) in each country and the bottom ten percent of lagging regions increased by 60 percent between 1995 and 2013. The same pattern emerges applies to the EU. On average, the frontier regions have grown by 1.7 percent per year, while both the bottom ten percent and the bottom 75 percent of lagging regions grew by around 1.4 percent a year. The growth gap may be small – on average 0.3 percentage points per year – but has accumulated over a period of 20 years. As a result, the gap in productivity levels between the frontier and the bottom ten percent increased by 56 percent between 1995 and 2014 (see Figure 1).[8] By 2014, this gap in terms of annual GDP per worker reached around €30,000 in constant prices and PPP. Indeed, the gap between the bottom 75 percent and the top ten percent increased

---

[6] Indeed, a key indicator of the transatlantic gap is productivity performance. For a summary, see Ortega-Argilés et al. (2015). They find that, across manufacturing, high-tech manufacturing and services, US firms are more able to translate their R&D investments into productivity increases (see also Badinger et al. 2016).

[7] As Krugman (1994) notes: 'Productivity isn't everything, but in the long run it is almost everything. A country's ability to improve its standard of living over time depends almost entirely on its ability to raise its output per worker.'

[8] Note that without Bulgaria and Romania, which entered the EU only in 2007, the increase would be 45 percent for the 1995–2014 period.

https://doi.org/10.1080/2578711X.2019.1547486

Figure 1   The increasing productivity gap between frontier and lagging regions in the EU, 1995–2014

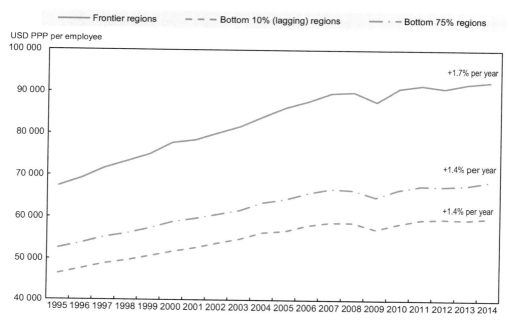

Source: OECD Regional database. Data at TL2 regional level.

even further (by 61 percent), indicating that 'leaders are breaking away from the pack' (OECD 2016e). This type of trend was empirically predicted at the turn of the millennium (see Cheshire and Magrini 2000), but did not trigger a sufficiently comprehensive response. Without a change, the bottom 75 percent of regions could fall to only about 48 percent of the productivity of the top ten percent by 2050, from the current 35 percent.

A consequence of this continued regional divergence is that most of the inequalities across EU countries are now accounted for by differences *within* rather than *between* countries.[9] The dispersion of both GDP per worker and GDP per capita across EU countries decreased significantly between 1995 and 2014, but not the differences within the countries (Figure 2). Using the Theil index, the total of inequality in the EU can be deconstructed into these 'within' and 'between' variations. In 1995, more than two-thirds of the inequality in GDP per capita within the EU28 was due to inequality between countries. By 2015, the within-country inequality contributed as much to total inequality as the between-country inequality. Put differently, the entire decline in inequality in Europe derives from a reduction of inequality across countries, while inequality within countries has actually grown.

---

[9] See, for example, McCann (2016) on how the United Kingdom's poor recent productivity performance is largely an urban and regional problem, with London having 'decoupled' itself from the rest of the UK economy. London's economic performance contributes to national averages that disguise weaknesses in other regions. See also Martin et al. (2017) on productivity growth paths of British cities.

https://doi.org/10.1080/2578711X.2019.1547486

Figure 2 Dispersion of productivity and GDP per capita across EU countries has reduced, but not across regions within countries, 1995–2014

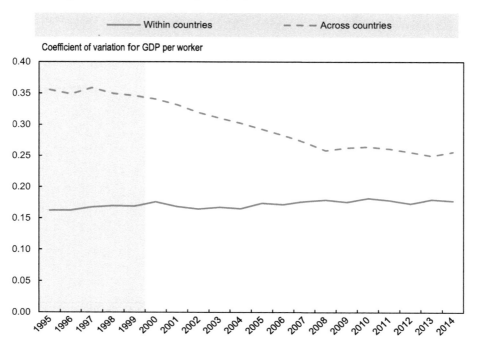

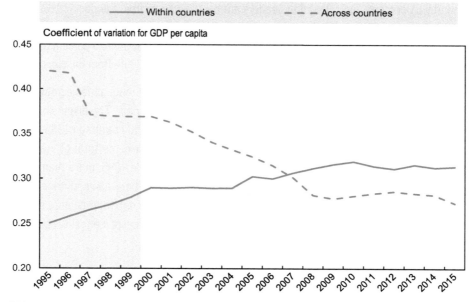

Source: OECD Regional database. Data at TL2 regional level.

          https://doi.org/10.1080/2578711X.2019.1547486

Thus, while EU market and economic integration has been a successful convergence machine for countries, these gains have not been distributed equally inside each country. Some regions have benefited more than others. By focusing on gaps in regional GDP per capita, the design of EU Cohesion Policy partly aimed to address these potential sources of divergence within countries, but the scope of the problem appears to have been underestimated, and the mechanisms driving these trends were not fully appreciated. Governments thought they could adapt to globalisation by focusing on sectoral policies (such as labour, education, skills, innovation, etc.) and by compensating the regions losing from the shocks for medium-term adjustment costs. However, this policy approach cannot fully address the sources of the problem.

While the full picture requires further analysis, a likely explanation for the asymmetric effects of globalisation at the regional level is as follows. Currently, approximately two-thirds of EU economies are in non-tradable sectors, many of which are located in large cities. Figure 3 displays the location of EU clusters by type of region. Mostly urban areas are characterised by non-traded activities or tradable sectors with high value-added (e.g. music, video, financial services, biopharma, aerospace). By contrast, agriculture and traditional manufacturing (e.g. footwear, leather, apparel, textiles and wood products) are mainly located in intermediate and rural areas.

Those people living in large cities are therefore benefiting from lower tradable prices and more imported product diversity, while, to some extent, being relatively sheltered from international competition. By contrast, rural areas and smaller-sized cities can only produce tradeable (or traded) goods because they do not have the density of population to be highly specialised in service sectors. Those territories in which these tradable sectors were concentrated were more directly affected by globalisation shocks. Further, the shocks in low-density areas were much more idiosyncratic than in cities. In large cities, there is constant creation and destruction of enterprises and employment. In low-density areas, the shocks are felt much more directly, and the scope for adjustment is much more limited. This adjustment problem cannot be addressed only by the mobility of people, which is much lower than standard economic models typically assume.[10] The sentiment of being left behind is perhaps one of the sources of the so-called 'geography of discontent' (see Los et al. 2017; Rodríguez-Pose 2017).

The important point is that such tensions at the regional level cannot be fully addressed by compensatory policies relying on income transfers. The adaptation to the specific shocks on regional economies generated by globalisation and market integration require differentiated (place-based or place-sensitive) strategies (Barca 2009; Bachtler and Begg 2018; Rodríguez-Pose 2017).

3.2 HOW REGIONAL DISPARITIES MAY AFFECT EU PRODUCTIVITY

Regional disparities have an impact on the aggregate productivity of countries. To explain this point, it is useful to categorise EU regions, for analytical purposes, according to their productivity performance

---

[10] Labour mobility has probably even decreased in the aftermath of the crisis, due to negative equity due to the fall of real estate prices or sunk costs associated with the housing crisis.

Figure 3 Share of total employment in EU clusters by type of region, 2016

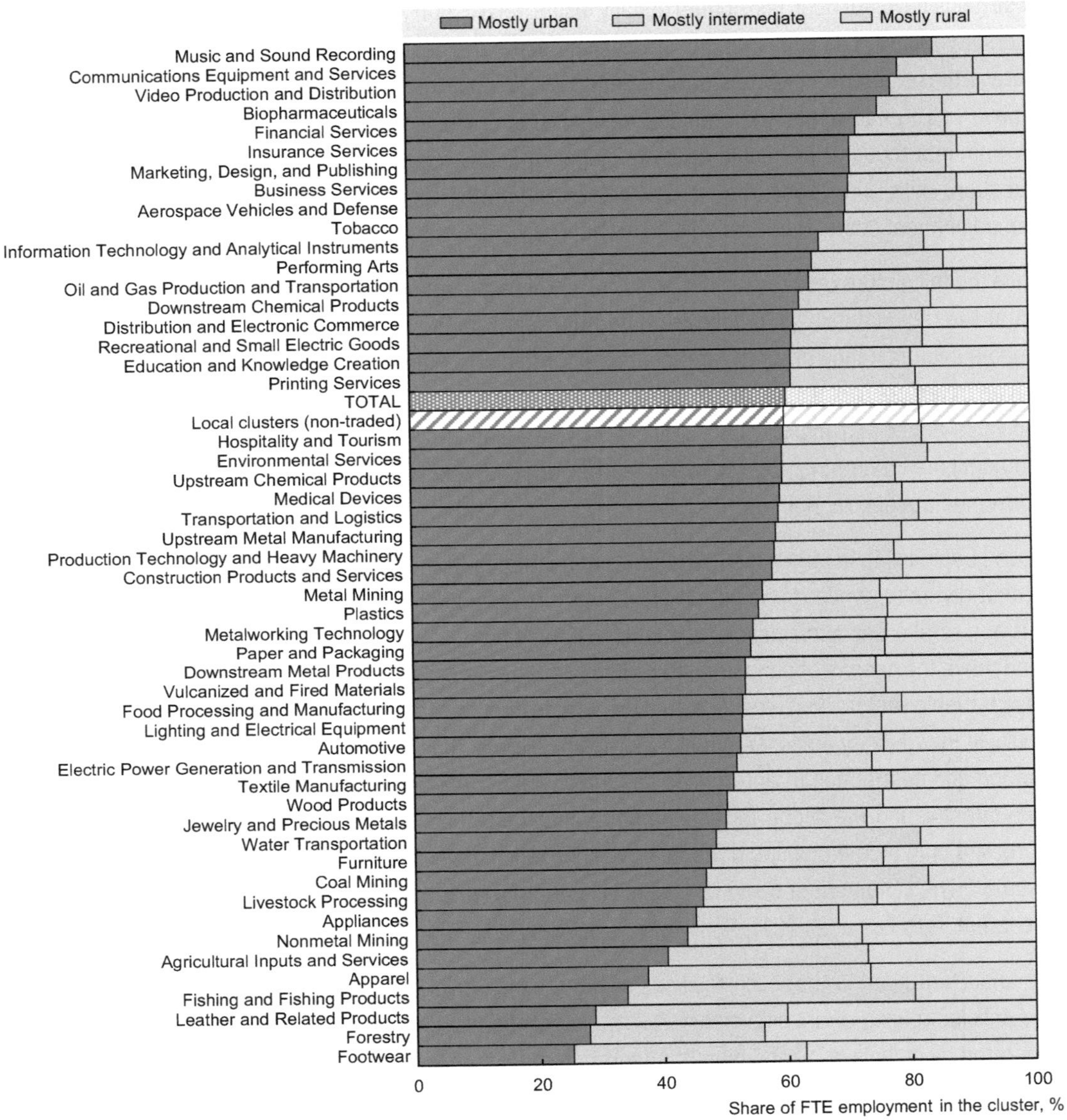
Mostly urban
Mostly intermediate
Mostly rural
Music and Sound Recording
Communications Equipment and Services
Video Production and Distribution
Biopharmaceuticals
Financial Services
Insurance Services
Marketing, Design, and Publishing
Business Services
Aerospace Vehicles and Defense
Tobacco
Information Technology and Analytical Instruments
Performing Arts
Oil and Gas Production and Transportation
Downstream Chemical Products
Distribution and Electronic Commerce
Recreational and Small Electric Goods
Education and Knowledge Creation
Printing Services
TOTAL
Local clusters (non-traded)
Hospitality and Tourism
Environmental Services
Upstream Chemical Products
Medical Devices
Transportation and Logistics
Upstream Metal Manufacturing
Production Technology and Heavy Machinery
Construction Products and Services
Metal Mining
Plastics
Metalworking Technology
Paper and Packaging
Downstream Metal Products
Vulcanized and Fired Materials
Food Processing and Manufacturing
Lighting and Electrical Equipment
Automotive
Electric Power Generation and Transmission
Textile Manufacturing
Wood Products
Jewelry and Precious Metals
Water Transportation
Furniture
Coal Mining
Livestock Processing
Appliances
Nonmetal Mining
Agricultural Inputs and Services
Apparel
Fishing and Fishing Products
Leather and Related Products
Forestry
Footwear
0
20
40
60
80
100
Share of FTE employment in the cluster, %

NB: Urban regions are those with at least 70 percent of the population living in Functional Urban Areas or part of the population living in a large metropolitan area of at least 1.5 million people.

Source: Calculations based on OECD Regional Statistics (2017) and data used and provided by Ketels and Protsiv (2016). Data at TL2 regional level.

 https://doi.org/10.1080/2578711X.2019.1547486

Table 1 Contribution of the different regional productivity patterns to aggregate EU GDP and employment growth, 2000–2014

	Contribution to EU GDP growth	Share of EU GDP 2000	Share of EU GDP 2014	Share of EU Employment 2000	Share of EU Employment 2014
Frontier regions	32%	22%	24%	18%	19%
Catching-up regions	24%	18%	19%	23%	22%
Keeping pace regions	30%	40%	38%	38%	39%
Diverging regions	15%	21%	20%	21%	21%

Source: OECD Regional database. Data at TL2 regional level.

into frontier regions, catching-up regions, keeping-pace regions, and diverging regions,[11] which usefully represent productivity performance within countries.

It is striking that the majority of GDP and employment in the EU (around 60–62 percent) were generated in regions that are either keeping pace or diverging (see Table 1 and Figure 4). Despite their large share in the economy, they only contributed 45 percent of the EU growth during the 2000–14 period. By contrast, the frontier regions, representing only 19 percent of employment, contributed 32 percent of the EU growth rate and accounted for 24 percent of GDP by 2014. The regional productivity of catching-up regions contributed 24 percent of EU economic growth. These regions increased their share of EU GDP to 19 percent, although their share of employment decreased slightly.

How can these different types of regional productivity dynamics be characterised in terms of their urban vs. rural nature? Figure 4 shows the percentage of regions in each category, which can be considered *mostly urban*, *intermediate* and *mostly rural*.[12] Not surprisingly, most of the frontier regions (above 90 percent) are primarily urban. These are regions with a high density of people and firms, where many high-value products and services are located.

---

[11] For a description of the method to establish this analytical classification, see OECD (2016c). The regional breakdown is based on the OECD Territorial Level 2 classification, corresponding broadly with the EU NUTS 2 level, as follows: **(i) Frontier regions** have the highest productivity levels *in each country*. In order to avoid the definition depending on special cases, the frontier regions in each country need to cover at least 10 percent of the population; **(ii) Catching-up regions** have reduced the productivity-level gap vis-à-vis the frontier regions during the period under consideration; **(iii) Keeping-pace regions** have maintained (±5%) the productivity-level gap vis-à-vis frontier regions during the period under consideration; and **(iv) Diverging regions** have increased the productivity level gap vis-à-vis frontier regions during the period under consideration

[12] TL2 (NUTS 2) regions have been classified as mostly urban (MU), intermediate (IN) or mostly rural (MR), according to the percentage of residents living in Functional Urban Areas (cf. OECD 2016c). Regions with more than 70 percent of their population living in a FUA, or some percentage of their population living in a large metropolitan area with more than 1.5 million inhabitants, are classified as mostly urban, and those with less than 50 percent are classified as mostly rural.

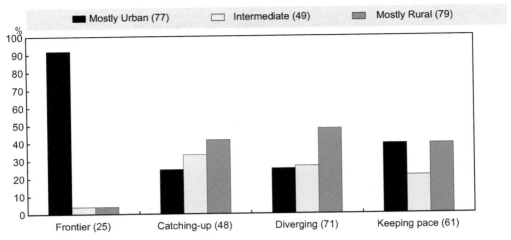

Note: In parenthesis, the number of regions in each category.

Source: OECD Regional database. Data at TL2 regional level.

Also predictable is that the majority of the diverging regions (48 percent) are mostly rural. However, less expected is that the highest share of catching-up regions (42 percent) is also mostly rural, in particular among those close to the cities. Conversely, around 25 percent of the diverging regions and 40 percent of the keeping-pace regions are mostly urban.

These figures show that productivity catching-up and underperformance are not necessarily associated with urban or rural characteristics. Examples of successes and problems can be found in all types of regions. It also follows from this that an urban or rural policy approach is not necessarily the most appropriate, given that, empirically, the performance of regions is more complex. Policy should focus on the linkages. Hence, as discussed below, a different policy approach and classification should be used if the EU is to deliver on the inclusive growth agenda.

3.3 DIFFERENTIATED REGIONAL PRODUCTIVITY CATCHING-UP WITHIN EU COUNTRIES

The impact of regional productivity catching-up on the aggregate productivity of countries can be illustrated by the contribution of each region to the aggregate GDP growth rate, as well as the regional contribution to the growth rate of national productivity.[13]

---

[13] The regional contribution to GDP growth is straightforward; it is the growth rate of each region between *t* and *t* + 1 multiplied by the share of that region in the national GDP. The contribution to aggregate productivity is more complicated because labour productivity is a ratio. Here, a counterfactual is used corresponding to what would have been the aggregate productivity without each given region. If in this counterfactual the aggregate productivity is higher than average, that means that a given region contributes negatively to the aggregate growth rate (for more details, see OECD 2016c).

Regional Studies Policy Impact Books   https://doi.org/10.1080/2578711X.2019.1547486

From this perspective, two types of countries emerge (see Annex 1 for individual country data).

Contribution to aggregate GDP growth rate vs. regional contribution to the growth rate

The first category (distributed productivity model) comprises countries such as Austria, Czech Republic, Germany, Italy, Poland, Portugal, Romania and Spain. In this group, most of the aggregate productivity performance is the result of the catching-up of the lagging regions. Frontier regions are typically major contributors to GDP growth because they are large, but they have much smaller or negative contributions to aggregate productivity growth. Put differently, frontier regions sustain high productivity levels, but productivity growth dynamics occur elsewhere in the country. Regional policy favouring the productivity performance of lagging regions acts as an important driver of a nationwide growth strategy.[14]

The second category (concentrated productivity model) includes countries such as Bulgaria, Denmark, France, Finland, Greece, Hungary, Netherlands, Slovak Republic, Sweden and the United Kingdom. In these countries, both GDP growth and aggregate productivity growth are dominated by the frontier regions. The aggregate growth is concentrated at the frontier with limited effects from the catching-up process. This strong territorial asymmetry signals that a growth potential may exist at the regional level that has not yet materialised or could be further mobilised. This should be the main task for EU and national territorial development strategies, recognising interdependencies among the performance of different territories.

The above suggests that there may be untapped potential to increase nationwide productivity by improving the performance of regions. This is the main argument underpinning the case for territorial/regional policy intervention. Indeed, governments should not address regional disparities based on territorial equity objectives alone, but as a way of addressing the faltering productivity growth of countries as a whole.

The main point is that the productivity divergence mainly takes place within certain countries, while there is a broad regional convergence pattern across the EU. To illustrate this point, Figures 5a and 5b illustrate the four types of regions according to the productivity dynamics: frontier, converging, 'keeping pace' and diverging. In Figure 5a, the frontier was calculated at the European level, by taking the top productivity regions across Europe. In order to avoid idiosyncratic cases, this group of frontier regions needs to account at least for ten percent of the EU population. It can be seen that most European regions are either converging or keeping pace vis-à-vis the EU frontier (see also, European Commission 2017e). This broad regional convergence, at least in part, can be related to the existence of an EU Cohesion Policy. Nevertheless, two countries in Europe still display a striking productivity divergence for most of

---

[14] Regional policy also has a role in unlocking the productivity growth of frontier regions in countries that are not converging; as the OECD team notes, the convergence of lagging regions in a country depends on the growth of the frontier regions in that country.

Figure 5a   Differences in productivity performance across the EU relative to EU frontiers,
2000–2014

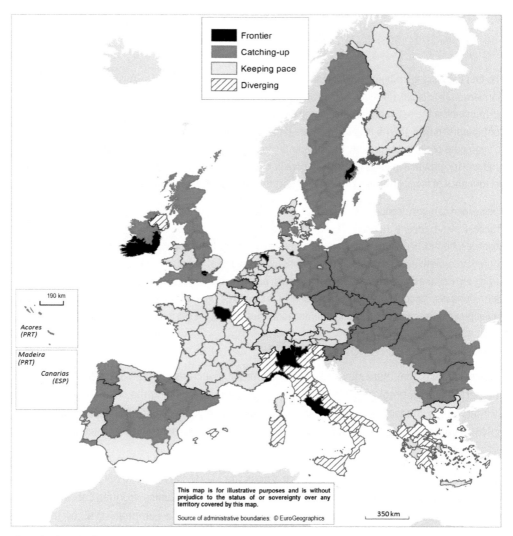

Frontier
Catching-up
Keeping pace
Diverging

190 km

*Acores
(PRT)*

*Madeira
(PRT)*

*Canarias
(ESP)*

This map is for illustrative purposes and is without
prejudice to the status of or sovereignty over any
territory covered by this map.

Source of administrative boundaries: © EuroGeographics

350 km

Note: Data for Croatia, Estonia, Latvia and Lithuania are not available. For the methodology underpinning the classification of regions for analytical purposes, refer to footnote 13.

Source: OECD Regional database.

their regions: Greece and Italy. The other diverging regions relative to the EU frontier are Northern Ireland (UK) and Champagne-Ardennes (FR).

By contrast, Figure 5b shows the same type of calculation but using a national productivity frontier rather than a European one (similarly, each national frontier needs to account for at least ten percent of the population). It turns out that many regions in Europe are diverging relative to their national frontiers. Namely,

https://doi.org/10.1080/2578711X.2019.1547486

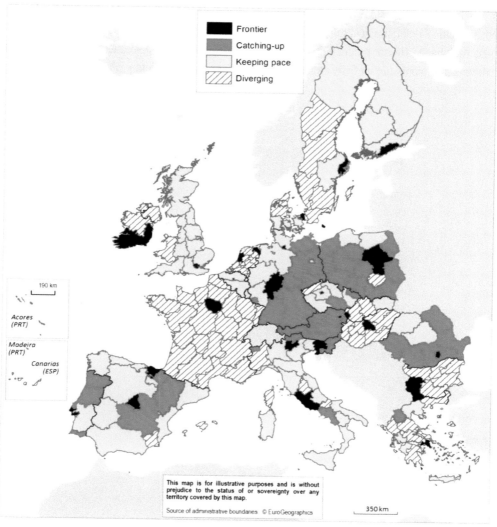

Note: Data for Croatia, Estonia, Latvia and Lithuania are not available. For the methodology underpinning the classification of regions for analytical purposes, refer to footnote 13.

Source: OECD Regional database.

most countries belonging to the concentrated productivity model display regional divergence. France is a particularly salient case with all regions diverging relative to Ile-de-France, where Paris is located. In the UK, most regions are keeping pace vis-à-vis Greater London, but this is not particularly good news, given that the UK has the largest regional productivity gaps across OECD countries. Even a country like Sweden, characterised by a rather inclusive society, sees most regions diverging or keeping pace vis-à-vis the region where Stockholm is located.

https://doi.org/10.1080/2578711X.2019.1547486

These figures suggest that despite the EU efforts to promote regional convergence, some European countries have adopted an aggregate productivity model that tends to exacerbate interregional productivity gaps. While it is not possible to establish a clear-cut relationship between economic conditions and increased political polarisation in the EU, it is likely that national societal consensus is negatively affected by these regional/territorial productivity disparities. At this point, the main questions are: what are the main drivers of regional productivity catching-up and what can policy do to promote them?

https://doi.org/10.1080/2578711X.2019.1547486

Comparison of regional performances relative to national and EU frontiers shows that there are groups of countries that have the best of both worlds, i.e. they are closing the gap with the European frontier while at the same time spreading the growth potential across their respective territories (Poland, Romania, Slovenia). Austria and Germany display similar trends, but most of their regions are already so developed that they are only keeping pace with the European frontier. Regions in the Czech Republic, Portugal, Spain and the United Kingdom are also managing to narrow the European productivity gap, but from a national perspective most non-frontier regions are only keeping pace with the national frontier. The unused regional growth potential however can be more clearly seen in countries like Bulgaria, Hungary, Ireland and Sweden, where non-frontier regions are growing reasonably well relative to the EU, but they are diverging relative to their national frontiers. On the other hand, France and the Netherlands, and especially Greece and Italy, display divergent trends at the national level, while also widening the European productivity gap or keeping pace at best.

Translating these different situations into policy responses is no easy task, as productivity growth interrelationships need to be taken into account. Some insights in this regard are provided by OECD (2015d), which shows that firms' aggregate productivity growth can be disentangled into contributions from firms at the global frontier, the national frontier, and firms lagging behind, with growth cascade of relationships (spillovers and adoption effects from global frontier down to laggard firms [Figure 6]).

This research indicates a similar cascade of relationships exists at the regional level. Taking a policy formulation perspective, there are global frontier regions, followed by intermediate regions that also include national frontiers that do not fall into the first group, and then, of course, regions that are lagging behind. Given systematically different sectoral structures, as shown in Figure 3, these regions perform different functions at the global and national levels (for example provision of global and national services), and as such they require different policy responses and diffusion mechanisms adapted to their specific territorial contexts (OECD 2016e).

4.1 STRATEGIES FOR GLOBAL FRONTIER REGIONS

As noted above, at the apex are the so-called global frontier regions, regarded as the drivers of innovation and growth, which, to varying degrees, should also pull other regions forward. These global frontier regions are generally urban regions containing very large cities or industrial 'powerhouses' such as Ile-de-France, Stockholm, Amsterdam and Copenhagen (OECD 2016e). They are already the most advanced as far as structural transformation is concerned, as they have efficient and effective ecosystems in place. They have state-of-the-art infrastructures, especially those related to knowledge such as research facilities and ICT, and world-class knowledge institutions. They also have a critical mass of competitive and dynamic firms and access to talent with well-established linkages both locally and internationally; their well-developed institutions are characterised by enhanced collaboration, joint investment, risk-taking, experimentation, efficient educational and training systems, etc.

While they have many self-sustaining mechanisms – and are often the main beneficiaries of (supposedly aspatial) national sectoral policies for infrastructure, education, R&D and employment – sustaining their

https://doi.org/10.1080/2578711X.2019.1547488

performance in a European context is important for the competitiveness of the EU as a whole, and for their transformation from European to global 'champions' (Roland Berger 2014).

The competitive advantage of global frontier regions is not just, or even primarily, in their investments in knowledge-based capital, but in 'how they tacitly combine different types of intangibles in the production process' (OECD 2015d: 26). Specifically, it depends on how efficiently their ecosystems function, and how well they are able to compete and cooperate at the same time. However, it is in the common European interest, including all the other regions, that the global frontier regions are also empowered to position themselves at the top of the global competitiveness charts. Key policy requirements include:

Global frontier regions must position themselves at the top of the global competitiveness charts, by

- implementing outstanding structural and regulatory reforms, which may be horizontal (EU or national), but which are especially crucial for these regions – issues such as standardisation, data protection, laws enabling provision of the sharing economy and new business models, digital security;
- reinvigorated and more focused implementation of excellence-based instruments and investments (e.g. Horizon 2020), such as research and ICT infrastructures, skills development and mobility, and knowledge flows;
- strengthening links to other regions to develop (geographically based or virtual) value networks or creating synergies among ongoing and new initiatives such as the Vanguard Initiative, the Smart Specialisation Platform for Industrial Modernisation, or the Knowledge and Innovation Communities of the European Institute of Technology (European Commission 2016a); and
- increasing the capacity to manage inclusion, given that many frontier cities, are characterised by polarised labour markets, are magnets for migrants and face serious challenges of social exclusion.

4.2 STRATEGIES FOR INTERMEDIATE REGIONS

The second group comprises intermediate regions. These are regions that are directly related and linked to the global frontier and have the capacity to follow, to varying degrees, but are capable of performing much better, if the European 'regional catching-up machine' were more effective (OECD 2016e). This regional productivity catching-up is often associated with borrowed agglomeration effects from large cities[15] or the presence of tradable sectors that sustain 'unconditional' convergence (see OECD 2018).

Examples of such regions include Piedmont or Umbria in Italy, as well as a number of regions outside the capital areas in developed countries from France and Sweden to Ireland and Belgium, including

---

[15] Proximity to cities is usually defined as a 1-hour time distance to a large urban centre.

regions such as Burgenland and Kärnten in Austria. In the case of lagging countries, these intermediate regions also tend to perform the role of the national frontiers, such as the cases of Madrid (ES), Attiki (EL), Mazovia (PL), Ljubljana (SI) or Lisbon (PT); the category also includes regions lagging behind the national frontiers, such as Castilla y León in Spain.

For the intermediate regions, the process of catching-up or narrowing the gap with the frontier regions requires them to transform themselves from 'global frontier suppliers' into leading creators of (distinct) value within the global networks, thus strengthening and expanding value-added in their tradable sectors. It is within such networks that learning and diffusion processes from the global frontier to the intermediate regions can take place, and similarly from the intermediate regions to the lagging regions. The OECD (2015d: 27) underlines the importance of understanding the barriers to the diffusion of unexploited existing technologies, which are the 'key in understanding cross-country differences in aggregate performance', especially due to differences in penetration rates, which are increasing over time (Comin and Mestieri Ferrer 2013).

In order to promote diffusion, the OECD (2016e: 30) has argued that:

> The shift in the global frontier can be transmitted to national frontiers through the mobility of production factors (capital, labour) and trade flows. Within countries, the investment in knowledge-based capital and all actions favouring spillovers and adoption may facilitate the diffusion of the frontier innovations to lagging firms, sectors or regions. This process is facilitated by a macro-structural environment that supports, rather than hinders, the shift of resources across sectors and the upscaling of best productivity practices.

The European Commission (2017a, 2017b, 2017c) has also provided extensive evidence why such challenges and barriers need to be addressed in a comprehensive and integrated, but regionally differentiated, manner, i.e. enforcing structural reforms in conjunction with RTDI, ICT, human capital, business, institutional and other policy measures in a territorially adapted and mutually consistent development strategy framework. It should be borne in mind that it is only at the regional level (although in some cases at the local level as well, depending on the scale) that the ecosystems referred to in Chapter 2.3 can be set up.

Strengthening and broadening the *catching-up process* among firms, industries and regions though setting up ecosystems conducive to the requirements of the fourth production revolution can contribute most to aggregate growth as the frontier contributes less than a third of the EU's GDP growth (OECD 2016b). Consequently, it is the non-frontier regions, both intermediate and lagging, that should be at the heart of policies for the structural transformation and inclusive growth agenda of the EU.

4.3 STRATEGIES FOR LAGGING REGIONS

Further away from both global and intermediate regions are the lagging regions. Their catching-up performance depends mainly on the intermediate (and national frontier) regions, i.e. regions of the European periphery in the east and south, plus (some) outermost regions. The greater the distance of a

Regional Studies Policy Impact Books   https://doi.org/10.1080/2578711X.2019.1547488

region from the frontier, the greater are the challenges of transformation and setting up efficient ecosystems. In particular, some rural remote regions have a particularly bleak productivity performance.

This is not just because these regions tend to be institutionally weaker (European Commission 2017a), but also because the structures of their economies are much more specialised in agriculture and traditional, more standardised manufacturing, and they are, as a consequence, exposed to stronger idiosyncratic shocks (see Chapter 3.2 above). That said, it is critical that the lagging regions participate in the structural transformation agenda and develop regional (innovation) ecosystems. This policy mix is in principle no different to the one for the intermediate regions (European Commission 2017a), with the caveat, of course, that they have different starting positions that should be taken into account and that their catching-up process should thus be geared towards intermediate regions as suggested by the OECD (2015d). There are however, considerations that tend to require two specific additional policy interventions.

First, there are infrastructure gaps that need to be addressed in areas such as ICT network infrastructure (i.e. address the digital divide between urban and rural areas), environmental infrastructure (especially in rural areas), and national transport network infrastructure (apart from TEN-Ts), where the focus is on connecting the economic growth centres (cities) with each other and hinterlands to generate spillovers. The latter is simply logical policy-making, as proximity to cities has been shown (see Chapter 2.3) to be one of the key growth drivers of such regions (OECD 2014; Ahrend and Schumann 2014; OECD 2016e).

This needs, however, to be nuanced, given the record of significant investment to date (particularly through EU funding) and questions over the cost-benefit and impact of some projects. As the European Commission (2017a: 46) has noted, 'infrastructure investment should be made limited in time, respond to clear criteria of need and development potential'. This also means that they should only be approved when implemented in conjunction with complementary activities (e.g. training and investment in productive capacity). As far as the needs are concerned, it has been shown that there are large differences among the lagging countries and regions; in particular, the transport endowments of low-growth regions tend, on average, to be much better than in low-income regions. Although gaps may exist in the low-growth regions that could justify investment, this should be considered an exception to the rule. However, for the low-income regions, the significant gaps indicate that infrastructure will still need to feature, at least to a certain extent, in their development strategies.

A particular challenge faces remote rural lagging regions. The evidence suggests that rural regions close to a city exhibit sound growth performance and that they should (in many cases) have good future prospects, at least when nearby cities perform well (OECD 2016e). For the less accessible rural regions, however, challenges of very low density and low accessibility put them in a different position. This is not to say that there are no opportunities: the evidence suggests that some of these regions perform well, and it is exactly through structural transformation and digitalisation that additional opportunities will become available (e.g. e-health, e-learning, e-business).

The focus of these areas however needs to be on finding the absolute (and not just relative) comparative advantage (OECD 2016e; OECD 2018), which is in practice harder to achieve as it requires even stronger specialisation, which in turn is associated with greater risks. Further, even though opportunities may increase in absolute terms, the regions could still be losing out in relative terms to the rural areas close to a city and other regions. This suggests a longer and more gradual transition towards structural trans-formation, with a need to capitalise on softer and more standard business opportunities (e.g. through standard business development support measures, growth of the tourism industry, stronger emphasis on community-based and institutional development, etc.).

4.4 THE CASE FOR AN INTEGRATED SYSTEM APPROACH FOR REGIONS AND CITIES

The key conclusion is the need for a consistent and mutually enforcing policy framework for different levels to function as a system. This is not just due to the cascade of interrelationships among different levels, but also because there are systemic interdependencies.

Regional productivity catching-up is not incompatible with very dynamic frontier regions. On the contrary, as shown by the OECD (2016e), 'most of the regions with high productivity growth rates have benefited from the potential pulling effect of the frontier region(s) to which they have converged'. Fast-growing frontiers thus mean much greater propensity for the productivity of other regions also to grow faster. Many Portuguese regions, for example, experienced strong productivity growth alongside the strong growth of the country's frontier, with Lisbon being an exception to the rule, i.e. with the frontier having a relatively small effect. By contrast, among the worst-performing regions, most of their poor productivity performance is the combined result of low performance of the national frontier region(s) and the lack of catching-up (with the exception of the Netherlands).

Therefore, it is critical for any strategy that promotes catching-up among the lagging regions to 'consider the system of regions when analysing and designing policies … ensuring that the frontier regions play fully their role and continue to perform' (OECD 2016e: 37). The same kind of interdependence can be seen from linked regional and national performances as identified in the EU Regional Innovation Scoreboard (European Commission 2016b).

Further the integrated territorial approach needs to be consistently embedded in the European policy mix and more focused on delivering key priorities. Sectoral policies cannot deliver on the promised EU agenda without the integrated territorial policy packages. The converse also applies; integrated territorial policy approaches without well-designed sectoral and structural policies and reforms cannot deliver prosperity and inclusive growth in the regions.

5. DEVELOPING A EUROPEAN POLICY RESPONSE

The starting point for a European policy response is that existing strategies – from Lisbon/Gothenburg to Europe 2020 – have been only partially successful with limited results in relation to the scale of the challenge. Recognition of the different starting points and potentials of regions in Europe is critical to a new structural transformation strategy. Only through a multi-layered approach is it feasible that all parts of the EU can successfully transform and thus achieve the inclusive growth objective based on improved productivity, EU-wide, and to the benefit of all EU citizens.

5.1 LESSONS FROM LISBON AND EUROPE 2020: PRINCIPLES FOR A NEW EU STRATEGY

The Lisbon Strategy was launched in 2000 with the strategic goal of the EU becoming 'the most competitive and dynamic knowledge-based economy in the world' (European Council 2000). Reviewed in 2005 on the basis of the Kok report (2004), the strategy was superseded in the late 2000s by Europe 2020. Although it has been characterised as a failure, the Lisbon Strategy provided important lessons for EU-level strategic policy-making (European Commission 2005, 2010a).

While Lisbon reflected a public consensus on the need for reforms to promote growth, the goals were overambitious. Despite some progress, most objectives were not achieved, particularly the closure of the productivity gap (European Commission 2010a). The strategy focused on some key areas of reform – RDTI, labour markets, business environment and consolidation of public finances – but neglected other elements such as stronger supervision of financial markets and macroeconomic imbalances (see also Mabbett and Schelkle 2007). Funding was limited largely to Structural and Cohesion Funds, with an overemphasis on expenditure and compliance at the expense of outcomes (Mendez et al. 2011; Begg 2016). Insufficient attention was given to the contributions of other parts of the EU budget and coherence with national policies (European Commission 2010a; Haase 2015). Lastly, progress was held back by weak governance, lack of influence of the 'Integrated Guidelines' approach, and weak political ownership within the European Council and the Member States (Tilford and Whyte 2010; Zgajewski and Hajjar 2005).

The successor Europe 2020 strategy was initially proposed by the Commission in March 2010, as a ten-year strategy for smart, sustainable and inclusive growth with five EU headline targets relating to the employment rate, research and development, climate change and renewable energy, education and poverty and social exclusion, and monitoring of progress through the European Semester.

Progress has been made in some areas, but the achievement of targets has been significantly affected by the crisis. Attainment of targets relating to greenhouse gas emissions and energy efficiency were 'aided' by the crisis in reducing overall energy consumption (Dijkstra and Athanasoglou 2015), while indicators relating to poverty and employment worsened (European Commission 2014b). There are also major differences across countries: Southern European countries are lagging behind, particularly in relation to the indicators related to employment, poverty and R&D, in comparison with many Central and Eastern European countries which have made better progress than EU15 countries such as France and Germany (Balcerzak 2015).

Regional Studies Policy Impact Books

https://doi.org/10.1080/2578711X.2019.1547489

However, the Europe 2020 strategy is hampered by the same weaknesses that affected the achievement of the Lisbon Strategy noted above.

Overall coordination and enforcement have been weak. National indicators, where available, were set by the Member States independently of EU-wide targets[16] and are not comparable in their levels of ambition (Daly 2012; Dijkstra and Athanasoglou 2015; European Commission 2015c). The enforcement method based on Country-Specific Recommendations and the European Semester, which largely relies on 'peer pressure', has been ineffectual (Van Rompuy et al. 2017; Council of the European Union 2014; Delmas 2015). The collective EU and Member State effort is clearly not adequate: for example, R&D expenditure continues to be largely concentrated in a handful of NUTS 2 regions in Northern and Central Europe,[17] with strong regions maintaining their leadership position and laggards not seeming able to catch up (Eurostat 2016). Importantly, the visibility of the strategy on the ground and stakeholder commitment are weak (European Commission 2015c).

Looking forward, any new EU strategic approach needs to recognise the lessons from the past and be realistic about what can be achieved. With relatively limited budgetary resources at EU level, it is widely acknowledged that the EU will need to establish the following principles for a new EU strategy.

Principles for a new UE strategy

- Focus on a limited number of key priorities that collectively promote accelerated innovation, structural transformation and inclusive growth. This needs to be articulated in a vision that begins with a strong, compelling narrative of the opportunities and challenges, and specifies what the desired outcomes should be (OECD 2016a).
- Encourage more effective and efficient governance to ensure institutional coordination and integration horizontally across the policy domains at EU, Member State and regional levels, and vertically between EU, national and regional levels (OECD 2011, 2016c; Pilat and Nolan 2016). The policy silos that generate trade-offs 'have become luxuries that our economies can no longer afford' (Francesca and Sylvain 2010; OECD 2011). Key EU policies requiring intensified policy coordination are: RTDI and ICT; human resource development; entrepreneurship; internationalisation and participation in global value chains; infrastructure development; and urban, rural and other territorial policies.
- Promote structural reforms and investment in institutional capacity to optimise the conditions for reform and investment (OECD 2013b), particularly in the key areas of labour market regulations,

---

[16] Member States did not have to set national targets and were not required to coordinate with other countries. The exception was GHG emissions and renewable energy, 'for which all Member States have set binding targets in a coordinated manner so that the sum of the national targets is equal to or higher than the EU targets' (Dijkstra and Athanasoglou 2015: 5).

[17] In Germany (10), the UK (4), Sweden (4), Austria (4) Finland (3), Denmark (2), Belgium (2) and Slovenia (1) (Eurostat 2016).

> wholesale and trade market regulations (see D'Costa et al. 2018). These factors of structural flexibility also promote the catching-up of the lagging regions. Other issues that need to be addressed are barriers to upscaling and upgrading, regulations regarding openness and global factor mobility, especially of knowledge flows, standardisation and an investment-friendly fiscal framework.
>
> - Ensure territorial and social inclusion, by taking account of territorial differences in the formulation and implementation of policies – 'bundles' of policy measures across different government levels need to be not just coordinated but also differentiated across different territories given their differing characteristics (although pursuing the same kind of goals) (Barca 2009).

Given the mixed results of past strategies, it is arguable that the EU needs greater mobilising power. This is underscored by the broad literature on structural transformation and the fourth production revolution discussed in Chapters 2 and 3 that advocate concerted action within Europe with coordinated European and national initiatives. For example, Kroll et al. (2016) make a convincing case for strengthened policy coordination with improved advanced manufacturing technologies ecosystems through better alignment of EU, national and regional policies, where the European level should focus on connecting, providing platforms and leverage synergies, while arguing for place-based (industrial) development at the national and regional levels.

It is only through a consistent, multi-layered approach that the EU will be able to capitalise on the opportunities of the fourth production revolution. In short, regulations, standards and structural reforms are critically needed, but can represent only part of the policy response. The missing links are the ecosystems, which can only be delivered at national and regional levels.

For the most important areas of EU policy intervention, there is clearly a need for a common European agenda for structural transformation setting out a joint vision, objectives and activities. This needs to ensure that the different policies are working in concert to combine both top–down (EU, national) and bottom–up (regional, national) policy interventions. In particular, it is essential that the policy framework is capable of mobilising integrated policy support at the most appropriate territorial level (which will vary between Member States) to ensure that the structural transformation agenda is adapted to different development contexts. Further, intensified structural changes will continue to have negative side effects (dislocation, inclusion, etc.) that need to be addressed through targeted and integrated territorial approaches in the specific regions affected.

The following sections discuss the contribution of the two main sets of policy levers at the disposal of the EU: the directly managed policies for infrastructure, research, SMEs and investment; and the role of Cohesion Policy. The role of economic governance – a key element of a new structural transformation agenda – is also considered.

5.2 FOCUS AND COHERENCE: IMPROVING THE EFFECTIVENESS OF DIRECT EU SPENDING

The EU budget has a crucial role in delivering well-targeted interventions, where the following framework conditions are met.

- *Investment in EU-wide infrastructure,* where there is a clear case for intervention on the basis of economies of scale, support for coordinating or mobilising national action or completion of 'missing links'. This includes research infrastructure (European Strategy Forum on Research Infrastructures), the development of the EU's ICT backbone network, and the TEN-T core network corridors.
- Pan-European *cooperation, networking and EU-wide mobility* schemes facilitating collaboration and engagement through, for example, joint research (Horizon 2020[18]) and knowledge exchange (Erasmus+, Marie-Curie Fellowships).
- *Common policy challenges* that require strongly coordinated EU-level action combined with pooling of finance from multiple countries, including policies that are reactions to sudden changes such as migration, defence, security and environmental threats.

Intervention in these areas has grown over the past two decades, with increasing direct spending on infrastructure, research and innovation, SME competitiveness and investment projects. Budgetary allocations to Heading 1a (competitiveness/internal market) have increased from an estimated 6.8 percent of the Multiannual Financial Framework (MFF) 2000–06 to 13.1 percent in the MFF 2014–20. The major programmes in the 2014–20 period under Heading 1a are shown in Table 2, highlighting the key programmes contributing to structural change – CEF, COSME, EaSI, Erasmus, EFSI and Horizon 2020 – which collectively account for allocations of almost €153 billion in the 2014-20 period. (An increase of €1.4 billion was proposed by the European Commission in the Mid-Term Review.)

Table 2   Major directly managed EU programmes, 2014–20

Major programmes	Key objective	Total allocation (€mill)
Connecting Europe Facility	Trans-European networks	21,937
Copernicus	Earth Observation Platform	4,291
Competitiveness of Enterprises	SME development	2,298
Customs, Fiscalis, Pericles, Hercule III	Effective customs union, anti-fraud, counterfeiting	908
Employment & social innovation (EasI)	Employment and social reforms	919
Erasmus+	Skills, education, employability	14,775
European Fund for Strategic Investments	Mobilising new investment	33,500
Galileo	EU satellite navigation system	7,072
Horizon 2020	EU global competitiveness	79,402
International Thermonuclear Exp. Reactor	Nuclear fusion as energy source	2,986
Nuclear decommissioning	Decommissioning nuclear plants	225
Wif4EY	Public wireless connectivity	120

Source: Based on European Commission (2016e, 2016f).

---

[18] In the proposals for the 2021–27 MFF termed Horizon Europe.

These programmes have seen strong take-up, with applications exceeding the available budget, in particular under Horizon 2020 and CEF, and are regarded as generating important added value and contributions to EU targets (European Commission 2016e, 2016f, 2016g). However, from the perspective of the structural transformation agenda, several important improvements are required.

- First, these programmes require a coherent performance framework to enable a systematic and comparable assessment of progress and strategic achievements across policy areas. Where evaluations are already available, a common concern is the lack of reliable data for assessing programme indicators and their achievements, including for their predecessor programmes (Steer Davies Gleave 2011; Ramboll 2015; Ernst and Young 2016). Studies also show considerable differences in the effectiveness of programmes; evaluations of past programmes show mixed results, with some programmes such as FP7 or Erasmus clearly outperforming others, such as the Trans-European Transport Network (TEN-T).
- Second, the additionality of programme spending is unclear. This applies particularly to EFSI, where the only evaluation conducted to date shows a wide range of interpretations of additionality (Ernst and Young 2016). Some of these are questionable, including the suggestion that receipt of EIB funding for the first time indicates that EFSI support is additional (Furik 2016). Evaluation research echoes the views from stakeholders (especially national promotional banks) that 'some of the financed projects could have been financed without EFSI support' (Ernst and Young 2016: 4). Recent research and other assessments have noted important concerns about the rigour of assessments of additionality, the share of public vs. private investment that goes into projects, the possible overestimation of the impact of EFSI, and issues relating to the Fund's governance and transparency of project selection (European Investment Bank 2016; European Court of Auditors 2016). More broadly, claims of additionality and added value of other spending under Heading 1a appear anecdotal, even axiomatic in some cases (European Commission 2015b). Indeed, the European Court of Auditors stated that plans to increase the Fund 'were drawn up too soon and with little evidence that the increase is justified' (European Court of Auditors 2016). Thus, justifications for future spending post-2020 need to be based more clearly on evidence.
- Third, there are important interrelationships between spending on infrastructure, SME competitiveness, research and other objectives, but the coherence of policies and instruments needs to be given a higher political priority. Evaluation and academic research has highlighted the relatively low coherence between CEF (including its TEN-T predecessor), Horizon 2020 (including FP7) and investments made with Structural Funds (Steer Davies Gleave 2011; High-Level Expert Group 2015).

For example, at a strategic level, investments under the TEN-T programme can have 'a two-way effect' on the growth of lagging, more peripheral regions. While they bring markets closer and increase these regions' opportunities to compete with core areas, they can also drive human resources and economic activities out of these regions. What is required, therefore, is a coherent policy mix supplementing improved accessibility and connectivity with measures aimed at enhancing the local contexts and supporting internationalisation (Faiña et al. 2016). Some of the specific problems are attributed to the

https://doi.org/10.1080/2578711X.2019.1547489

Figure 6   Heading 1a allocations to Member States, excluding EFSI (€ million), 2014–15

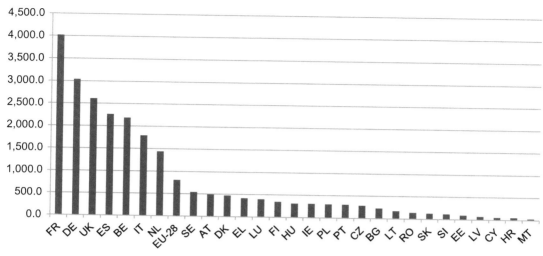

Note: Excludes EFSI projects expenditure.[19]

Source: DG Budget data.

institutional inability or unwillingness of different Commission DGs to cooperate (Steer Davies Gleave 2011), and the need for more synergies between spending on research and innovation via Horizon 2020 and other EU-wide programmes, as well as interventions supported by national science and innovation programmes (High-Level Expert Group 2015; Ferry et al. 2016). It has been argued that, without an 'effective policy mix', a high impact of publicly funded programmes cannot materialise (High-Level Expert Group 2015: 4). A long-standing problem of transport projects funded by TEN-T is that they are assessed and selected according to national rather than European priorities (Gutiérrez et al. 2011).

Lastly, the key message of this book is the need for all EU spending to take account of the territorial dimension, specifically how the intervention contributes to closing the gap between frontier, intermediate and lagging regions. Currently, the major beneficiaries of Heading 1a are large EU15 Member States. Drawing on data for 2014–15 (see Figure 6), spending on Competitiveness for Growth and Jobs was mainly in France, Germany and the United Kingdom, followed by Belgium, Spain, Italy and the Netherlands. By contrast, Central and Eastern European countries do not seem to have benefited from allocations of expenditure under this sub-heading. Under EFSI (see Figure 7), over 90 percent of funding (by mid-2016) had been allocated to projects in the EU15 Member States, especially Italy, France, the United Kingdom, Spain and Germany (Ernst and Young 2016).

---

[19] Contracts amounting to €10.4 billion were signed, but not spent, as of June 2016 (European Investment Bank 2016: 5).

https://doi.org/10.1080/2578711X.2019.1547489

Figure 7 Allocation of EFSI financing by Member State

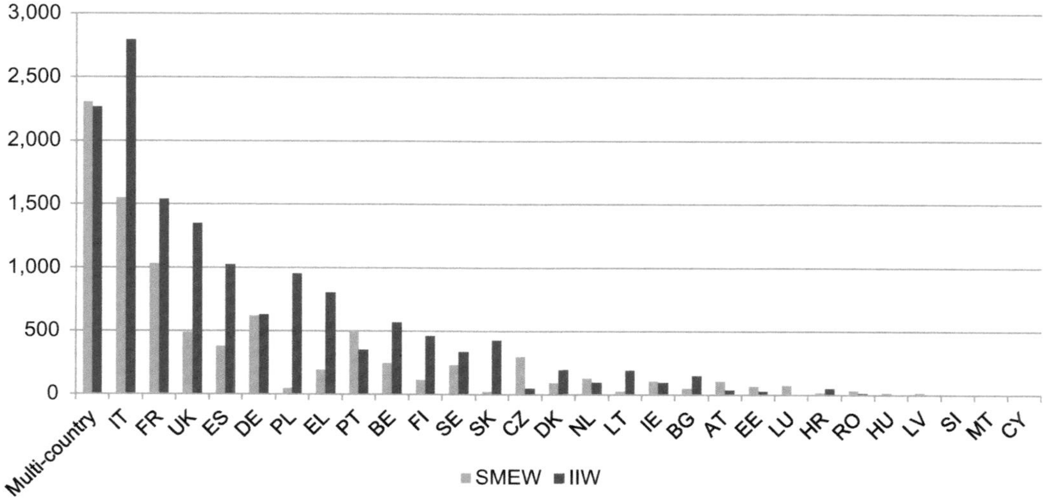

Note: Data are for total amounts of signed projects for SME Guarantee Window (SMEW) and Infrastructure and Innovation Window[20] (IIW) (€ million). Data are for April 2017.

Source: European Investment Fund (EIF) for SMEW and European Investment Bank (EIB) for IIW. EIF data available at: http://www.eif.org/what_we_do/efsi/ipe-efsi-geographies.pdf; EIB data available at: http://www.eib.org/efsi/efsi-projects/index.htm

In summary, directly managed policies have an important role to play, as they are well equipped to deliver targeted interventions, especially project-based ones. However, a priority for the post-2020 policy approach to structural change should be a more coherent strategic framework for the implementation of directly managed policies that takes into account their coherence with each other, with other headings and with the policies implemented in the Member State with own resources.

---

[20] For six IIW projects (3 from France, 2 from Germany and 1 from Spain) the financing sum for the projects was not publicly disclosed.

https://doi.org/10.1080/2578711X.2019.1547489

6. ENSURING TERRITORIAL AND SOCIALLY INCLUSIVE GROWTH: A MORE EFFECTIVE COHESION POLICY

In concert with more focused and coherent spending by the EU in areas such as research, SME competitiveness and infrastructure, and stronger economic governance and structural reforms, the EU needs powerful instruments to ensure that growth is territorially and socially inclusive. The success of a strategy for structural transformation depends on taking account of territorial differences in the formulation and implementation of policies as noted above – 'bundles' of policy measures across different government levels that need to be both coordinated and differentiated across different territories given their differing characteristics (but pursuing the same kind of goals).

EU expenditure under Heading 1b – Cohesion Policy – is currently the main EU policy instrument for economic, social and territorial cohesion. With a geographically discriminating allocation formula for funding, most of the funds distributed during 2014–2015 went to less-developed countries and regions. Poland, Spain, Italy, the Czech Republic and Hungary were the greatest beneficiaries of funding (see Figure 8).

Figure 8   Allocations of Heading 1b by Member State (€ million), 2014–15

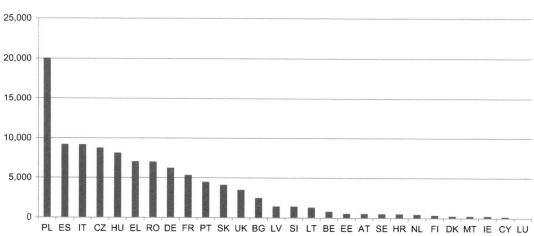

Source: DG Budget data 2016.

6.1 STRENGTHENING THE EFFECTIVENESS OF COHESION POLICY

In assessing the effectiveness of Cohesion Policy, the evidence base has historically been very mixed. During the 1990s and early 2000s, the strategies of Structural and Cohesion Funds programmes were often formulated in vague terms, with objectives only embryonically developed, and often disconnected from the outputs and results expected of programme measures (Bachtler et al. 2016, 2017). Several influential studies concluded that the policy had little or no impact in terms of reducing regional disparities (Boldrin and Canova 2001; Ederveen et al. 2006).

However, the past decade has seen improvements in the quality of Cohesion Policy programming and the rigour of evaluation (Polverari et al. 2014; Ward 2016; Davies 2017), and there is now a rich body

https://doi.org/10.1080/2578711X.2019.1547491

of evidence on which to judge the effectiveness of Heading 1b. The three main macroeconomic models applied to ESIF funding – QUEST, HERMIN and RHOMOLO – find clear positive effects in the net recipient Member States (both during programme implementation and in the longer term (Bradley and Untiedt 2009; Varga and in t'Veld 2010; Brandsma et al. 2013; Monfort et al. 2016). Micro-economic analysis and qualitative research on the specific objectives and instruments of programmes (using counterfactual evaluation) have found significant effects of ESIF in terms of the leveraging of private sector investment, business productivity, net job creation, and measures such as patent applications and transport infrastructure (Bondonio and Pellegrini 2016; Ward 2016; Bondonio and Martini 2012; Criscuolo et al. 2012; Alecke et al. 2010; Hart and Bonner 2011; Ferrara et al. 2017). The results from econometric regression analyses, which typically test for the effect of ESIF funding on convergence in GDP per capita, are more varied. While some studies find evidence that ESIF funding has a positive and statistically significant effect on convergence (e.g. Mohl and Hagen 2010; Becker et al. 2010), others find small effects (Esposti and Bussoletti 2008; Hagen and Mohl 2008) or no statistically significant impact on convergence (Dall'erba and Le Gallo 2008; Breidenbach et al. 2016). The variation in results is often critically dependent on the quality of national institutions or macro-economic policies (Beugelsdijk and Eijffinger 2005; Ederveen et al. 2006; Tomova et al. 2013).

Specifically with respect to structural transformation, Cohesion Policy has played a role in supporting regions in structural adaptation paths from the creation of the Funds, latterly fostering a shift from a productive model based on price to one based on innovation (CSIL et al. 2010). It has done so by supporting investments in human capital, regional specialisation, diversification of regional economies, innovation, competitiveness of local productive systems, and internationalisation. Traditionally, support was provided through subsidies for specific firms or types of firms, such as grants for restructuring or for foreign direct investment, or sectoral strategies (clusters) through a mix of aid to individual firms, dedicated infrastructure, and support and advice (Bachtler et al. 2016; Davies 2017).

Progress has, however, often been slow, especially in the period up to the mid-2000s. Many regions implemented strategies to support structural adjustment, but 'these activities were often slow to yield results, reflecting the difficulties in changing from established industries to new activities' (Bachtler et al. 2016: 82). Support to firms, for example, might have allowed firms to remain in the market, thus safeguarding jobs in the short/medium term, but it did not stimulate them to become more competitive for the longer term. In several regions, emphasis was placed on safeguarding jobs in industrial sectors where the long-term sustainability was questionable. In general, regions found it difficult to strike the right balance of support between: traditional sectors and new activities; short-term and long-term goals; and the economic and social aspects of structural adjustment. Strategies focused on innovation and internationalisation were most successful in supporting structural change. Support provided to firms at risk of closure impeded wider, longer-term structural change (Ward 2016). Again, institutions matter: 'the degree to which policy can contribute to structural change is not correlated with the historical regional specialisation on capital, equipment or traditional industries, but is highly correlated to the quality of the local institutions' (CSIL et al. 2010: 5).

In this context, the 2006 and 2013 reforms to Cohesion Policy were significant in transforming key aspects of the policy, relating to:

The 2006 and 2013 reforms to Cohesion Policy were significant, relating to:

- objectives, through thematic priorities aligned first with the Lisbon Strategy and latterly with Europe 2020;
- strategic coherence, through a common strategic and regulatory framework for all ESI Funds;
- a greater performance focus through results-orientated specification of objectives and outcomes, ex-ante conditionalities (EACs) and a performance reserve;
- greater potential leverage of spending through more use of financial instruments; and
- encouragement for integrated, localised, bottom-up development.

Initial assessments of the reforms introduced by the 2013 CPR to strengthen effectiveness are indicating that the new rules (e.g. EACs, programming architecture, thematic concentration and results-orientation) are having a positive effect on the focus of programmes. Programmes are now considered to be built on a 'more robust intervention logic' with a clearer connection between the aims of each intervention and how these will be achieved (Altus 2016; European Court of Auditors 2017), although the practical application is clearly difficult (European Court of Auditors 2018). More attention is being paid to ensure that the ESI Funds are coordinated with each other and with other EU policies (Altus 2016; Ferry et al. 2016). Importantly, a strategic approach to structural change is being encouraged through an obligation for each country/region to develop 'smart specialisation strategies' based on a twin-track strategy of consolidating existing traditional sectoral strengths through investment in key 'enabling technologies', while supporting related diversification into new innovative industries or activities. Integrated territorial development strategies are providing a more place-based policy response to the development needs of urban areas and other territories, with 'bundles' of interventions implemented through innovative and collaborative models of governance (Van der Zwet et al. 2017).

In assessing the post-2020 EU response to structural change, the experience to date has three sets of important lessons.

First, strategies for structural change need to reflect the comparative advantage of regions, which may well lie in traditional, low-tech rather than high-tech, innovative sectors. Identifying and tackling such comparative advantage requires a process that unearths the (often implicit) knowledge of stakeholders and civil society agents, along the lines of the quadruple helix model, and which transcends administrative silos (Kyriakou 2017; Kyriakou et al. 2017; Wostner 2017). Policies and strategies need to be designed with realism about the long-term timescale required for structural change; shifts in specialisation may take decades to achieve (CSIL et al. 2010, Bachtler et al. 2016). In this respect, critical mass is important. Thus, especially where the ESIF represent only a relatively limited amount of funding, it is essential that programme strategies are embedded in wider, longer-term policies (CSIL et al. 2010) with broader policy frameworks supporting innovation and entrepreneurship (Pelletier 2017).

Second, bold policies for structural transformation shifts need to be accompanied by equally bold social measures, capable of facilitating accelerated changes to education and skills and counteracting the

https://doi.org/10.1080/2578711X.2019.1547491

transitional social effects of the job losses in traditional industries. Again, the pursuit of synergies between different European Structural and Investment (ESI) Funds (European Social Fund (ESF) and European Regional Development Fund (ERDF), but also European Agricultural Fund for Rural Development (EAFRD) and European Maritime and Fisheries Fund (EMFF)) and social and welfare policies is paramount.

Third, the effectiveness of territorial policies for structural transformation depends on the quality of government and national and local institutions. They are important for setting the institutional context (recognised by the introduction of ex-ante conditionalities) for effective policy design (European Commission 2017d). In particular, they are necessary to facilitate the emergence of 'strategic vision, social entrepreneurship and collective risk-taking' (CSIL et al. 2010) and to change 'the way policy is done within government' (Wostner 2017). Effective development models also need to recognise that structural adjustment is a societal as well as an economic process. This requires the process of strategy development systematically to take account of the influence on performance of relevant societal or cultural constraints, and to build in institutional and social measures to address cultural, political or institutional conservatism and culture change (Bachtler et al. 2016: 121). The 'entrepreneurial discovery processes' realised under the 2014-20 ESIF programmes are a good example of how such a process of strategy development may be achieved, engaging civil society agents, creating value networks, and changing how stakeholders interact with each other (see Kyriakou 2017; Kyriakou et al. 2017; Wostner 2017). All these examples show why Cohesion Policy is vital in delivering ecosystems for the fourth production revolution.

6.2 THE EFFICIENCY OF COHESION POLICY IMPLEMENTATION

The complexity of implementation is one of the main weaknesses of Cohesion Policy. The administrative time and cost of implementing ESIF programmes have increased significantly, primarily due to the resources required for intensified financial management and control procedures (Mendez and Bachtler 2011; Davies 2015; Bachtler et al. 2017). The declining amount of Cohesion Policy funding in several of the more-developed EU Member States has led to claims that the management cost of Structural Funds programme administration is disproportionate to the scale of funding. Indeed, there is some evidence that the administrative workload in such cases is reducing the willingness of intermediate bodies and beneficiaries to take part in programmes. While there is widespread support for a major simplification of delivery systems and mechanisms, including fewer rules, regulations/acts and more legal certainty and proportionality, there are also structural barriers to such change due to the EU budgetary discharge requirements.

Steps were taken in 2013 to simplify aspects of administration, and some of these have clearly been beneficial, particularly in relation to simplified costs, flat rates, reporting requirements and e-cohesion (Davies 2015). However, measures have mainly benefited the workload of beneficiaries, and most managing authorities and intermediate bodies perceive that the regulations and accompanying acts and guidelines have become more complex and that the administrative workload and cost in managing the funds has increased.

The High-Level Group on ESI Funds Simplification was set up in 2015 to provide the Commission with advice on simplification measures and the reduction of the administrative burden for beneficiaries. Its agenda and outputs cover many important issues such as the single audit principle, proportionality and a more risk-based approach to controls, gold-plating of rules by national authorities and harmonisation of rules.

However, simplification can only go so far. There is increasing recognition at EU level of the need for a fundamental change to the management system for Cohesion Policy that goes beyond simplification of rules and recognises differences in institutional and administrative structures and capacities across Member States (Bachtler and Mendez 2016). The challenge will be to engineer a system that makes a real difference to administration. At the programming stage, it would need to ensure coherence with Cohesion Policy objectives and wider EU economic and industrial policies and provide a performance framework and a commitment to the principle of partnership. During implementation, there would need to be mechanisms for assurance on the regularity of spending, and evidence for the results achieved. The fundamental requirement is less onerous administrative requirements based on the key criterion of risk: those Member States (or programmes) that represent low risk – on the basis of scale of funding, national co-financing, record of implementation or proven capacity – could be subject to fewer controls.

Equally, continued application of shared management would be important in countries with larger amounts of EU funding and weaker administrative capacity. Cohesion Policy is credited with having strengthened administrative structures and cultures across Europe over successive periods through its programming requirements, and the focus on institutional capacity-building was reinforced in 2014-2020 by making it a thematic objective with dedicated funding (Mendez and Bachtler 2015).

As noted above, ex-ante conditionalities were introduced for the 2014–20 period in response to research showing that the effectiveness of Cohesion Policy spending was undermined by deficits in national/regional policy frameworks and institutional/administrative capacity. Member States have made considerable effort to comply with ex-ante conditionalities; Commission data indicate that 75 percent of ex-ante conditionalities were fulfilled at the time of programme approval, but with 750 conditionalities the subject of action plans. The principle of conditionalities has generally been seen as positive, especially in promoting awareness of the policy or institutional pre-conditions that need to be in place for effective implementation, and in influencing government departments/agencies to make the necessary legal, regulatory or organisational changes, despite the complexity of the process of compliance (European Commission 2017d).

Notwithstanding this initial experience, the quality of government varies significantly across the EU, and the evidence shows that institutional capacity-building and efficient public administration are particularly important for effective implementation of EU funding and where strong controls and Commission oversight continue to be warranted (Bailey and De Propris 2002; Rodríguez-Pose 2013; Charron et al. 2015). Indeed, there is a case for strengthening conditionalities related to the quality of government and administrative capacity as well as to strengthen the support for capacity-building.

That said, more radical approaches could also be conceived. Given the positive impact of ex-ante conditionalities, they could also take on the function of the present Operational Programmes, thus significantly reducing the administrative burden. Under such a scenario, the structure of ex-ante conditionalities should closely reflect the structure of the objectives of the reformed Cohesion Policy, which in practice means focusing on issues such as smart specialisation, inclusion and fulfilment of preconditions (transport, environment, energy). Delivery could

https://doi.org/10.1080/2578711X.2019.1547491

also be based on these conditionalities within the actual implementation process, i.e. payments could be made as bulk transfers of investment-conditioned grants (Wostner 2008) where national implementation systems provide sufficient assurance. In this case, however, the co-financing rates would presumably be lower. For the countries and regions where assurance is not sufficient, they could use simplified Joint Action Plans on the basis of ex-ante conditionality plans, simplified cost options or usual expenditure-based claims. In such cases, special ex-ante conditionality would refer to administrative and institutional strengthening.

6.3 ECONOMIC GOVERNANCE, EU SUSTAINABLE GROWTH AND STRUCTURAL TRANSFORMATION STRATEGY

Over the past three decades, Cohesion Policy has developed its own, unique system of multilevel governance, which has become a tangible and acknowledged landmark for the whole policy. Through programming and implementation, it allows the perspectives of different development partners to be reconciled, ranging from the European Commission, national governments, and regional and local institutions to private companies and civil society. The system has brought added value to socioeconomic and territorial management, including the development of partnership practices in all Member States. In some former centrally planned economies, it was even the major vehicle for developing modern policy-making capacities (including coordination, monitoring and evaluation) and the introduction of a multilateral system beneficial for all interactions across all levels of government, the private sector and NGOs.

As a major component of the EU budget, Cohesion Policy has increasingly needed to be responsive to EU policy goals and efforts to address major challenges, especially in the wake of the financial and economic crises. In institutional terms, this has meant greater linkage to the Europe 2020 strategy and the European Semester to assure alignment with EU macroeconomic and microeconomic policies. The changes to Cohesion Policy, introduced under the 2014–2020 MFF, were driven to a major extent by those expectations. As noted above, the whole programming structure of ESIF is aligned with the Europe 2020 strategy, and new features were added or further developed to support effectiveness and efficiency, including enforced concentration on EU objectives, macroeconomic and ex-ante conditionalities, performance frameworks, and the integrated territorial approach. A clear link was also made between Cohesion Policy and Country-Specific Recommendations issued by the Council under the European Semester process, which should guide structural reforms in Member States, though this link has proved less effective, notably due to the very short-term scope or lack of focus of CSRs.

The 2013 reforms strengthened the participation of some actors in Cohesion Policy decision-making (e.g. urban areas under ITIs or local actors under CLLDs) and extended the need for interactions between various partners in order to prepare and implement ex-ante conditionalities or meet targets set under the performance framework. However, they also shifted the focus of the governance system from using the indigenous capacities and potentials of a given territory to concentrate policy on realising EU goals and tackling challenges, which might be temporary or less relevant for a particular territory. These developments have changed the 'balance of power' within Cohesion Policy, eroding the bottom-up approach and subsidiarity principle and strengthening top-down, centrally and sectorally managed solutions.

https://doi.org/10.1080/2578711X.2019.1547491

In this way, Cohesion Policy has become an important instrument to realise different thematically defined goals (EU investment policy), but its capacity to respond effectively to new challenges that have territorial and far-reaching complex social and economic comprehensive effects is decreasing. The current policy may help to achieve clearly defined goals in some areas at EU level but at the expense of being less able to counter agglomeration effects fuelled by EU integration and globalisation. The reduced scope for a territorially based policy response may increase social inequality, amplify the threat of economic unintended effects (such as delocalisation of economic activities), and further undermine the development prospects of territories that are not well equipped with the pre-conditions for self-sustaining development.

Recent research findings (European Commission 2015b, 2017a, 2017c) clearly suggest that the results of Cohesion Policy depend on factors that can only be partially tackled inside Cohesion Policy. In other words, even the best policy programming and implementation systems are unable to overcome the negative effects of globalisation and integration in some territories if they are not complemented by effective coordination, policy-making and implementation systems, i.e. a comprehensive governance system with a clear territorial dimension.

The major external factors influencing the effective use of Cohesion Policy as a tool for bringing about structural change and greater economic and social cohesion across regions and localities of the EU include:

The major external factors include:

- governance – the level of decentralisation and the way in which interactions between different public institutions and development partners (private, social, others) are taking place, as well as the quality of institutions across all levels of government;
- the quality of European and national sectoral policies for supporting productivity (human resource development, education, export-oriented firms, innovation, infrastructure, essential public services) and their territorial differentiation; and
- the macroeconomic context, notably influences such as globalisation, the EU integration process, national fiscal policies, and demographic pressures.

As noted in the previous chapter, the current system of EU economic governance is only partly able to assist in creating the proper conditions for effective Cohesion Policy delivery. The focus is clearly on improving macroeconomic conditions and institutional reforms to help overcome persistent structural weaknesses in individual countries. CSRs are only partially relevant for improving the policy and institutional environment in which Cohesion Policy operates. Those CSRs relevant for Cohesion Policy relate mostly to the general policy context for investment (e.g. quality of public procurement or spatial planning) and the constraints on policy implementation solutions through incomplete structural reforms in (for example) labour markets, skills development, and education to improve human and social capital and employment opportunities.

Although the EU economic governance system helps to improve the dialogue between countries and EU institutions as well as the focus of national policies on crucial European reforms, it does not explicitly

https://doi.org/10.1080/2578711X.2019.1547491

focus on the opportunities for growth and employment in individual countries and regions. In part, this is because of the implementation method (open method of coordination), which requires a strong political commitment from national authorities to implement recommendations (without incentives or – in the majority of cases – sanctions), and also partly because of the absence of the territorial dimension in this exercise. Simply put, CSRs are formulated vaguely, with sectoral and short-term perspectives. They are, therefore, unable to promote sustainable development and an integrated approach in exploiting the different potentials of individual territories within the EU.

An ambitious sustainable growth and structural transformation strategy will require a stronger system of economic governance. This would identify the necessary long-term strategic adjustments (policy standards and reforms) to achieve set objectives and targets at the level of EU policies, countries and relevant sub-national levels. Under such a strategy, the Country-Specific Recommendations would become more structural, multi-annual and more oriented towards helping to enhance structural transformation at all levels of the EU governance system. As such, they would cover the steps necessary to support implementation of the structural transformation strategy at national but also at European, regional and local levels. In this context, some CSRs would have territorial implications – recognising the need to differentiate structural reforms, according (for example) to the distinctive development situation (development paths, opportunities, challenges) of frontier, catching-up and lagging regions, as well as the overall macroeconomic situation of the country concerned.

The following elements of the European Semester process would need to be redefined and refocused as follows.

- Country Reports. Prepared by the Commission and adopted by the Council, the Country Reports should focus primarily on analysing the actors influencing the ability of each country to achieve the goals and targets defined in the EU sustainable growth and structural transformation strategy. This should include an assessment of potentials and needs for the effective implementation of the structural transformation strategy and territorial disparities. Strategic Country Reports should be prepared every 3–4 years; those prepared on an annual basis should be regarded as a monitoring report with limited scope to introduce new proposals for reforms.
- National Reform Programmes (NRP). Prepared by each Member State, these should be converted into a medium-term programming document showing the steps and structural reforms needed to realise the strategic goals defined in the new EU strategy and taking account of the socioeconomic and territorial situation set out in Country Reports. Each NRP would also define actions to be undertaken in order to implement fully structural transformation strategy at national as well as relevant subnational levels. Converting a National Reform Programme into a real, multiannual strategic programming document would allow identification of the instruments available under various EU policies (not only Cohesion Policy) and national policies to realise proposed reforms and actions and forming the strategic coordination framework for various funds. The various documents used to programme individual EU policies (e.g. Partnership Agreement under Cohesion Policy) could therefore be reduced and their focus shifted from strategic analysis (part of new National Reform Programmes) to implementation issues. The preparation

of Country Reports and National Reform Programmes at the start of the 2021–2027 programming period would identify the most urgent and important reforms as well as the investment priorities to be realised under EU and national policies.

- Country Specific Recommendations (CSRs). Given the multiannual and strategic focus of the Country Reports and National Reform Programmes, the CSRs should similarly evolve in the same direction. CSRs should focus on the strategic reforms needed to achieve EU sustainable growth and structural reform, including those related to territorial matters and structural transformation. They should be more precisely defined, with concrete steps and timetables for implementing necessary reforms, and provide encouragement for implementation through a financial incentive scheme. Non-compliance with those strategic CSRs by a Member State would mean serious consequences, but these should not be related to particular EU funds – avoiding the kind of linkage made between macroeconomic condition- alities and ESIF. Instead, the penalties of non-compliance should be of a broader and more strategic nature that ensure fair treatment across all Member States. CSRs relating to implementation issues should be avoided – recommendations of this type should be defined at the policy level (e.g. Cohesion Policy) and implemented through mechanisms such as ex-ante conditionalities system under ESIF.

As noted above, Cohesion Policy has developed its own, unique system of instruments to support the achievement of goals ranging from thematic concentration (including earmarking of funds) through ex-ante conditionalities to a performance framework allowing policymakers to focus attention on the tangible results of the policy. This system – and ex-ante conditionalities in particular – has a direct influence on the qual- ity of the national and sub-national programming and delivery of Cohesion Policy (European Commission 2017d) by linking the allocation of funds to the implementation of EU legislation, the preparation of long-term visions, strategies and programmes and the creation or improvement of institutional capacity.

However, even full implementation of ex-ante conditions, the strict observation of concentration rules and full achievement of targets under performance frameworks do not provide assurance that countries and regions will improve their competitiveness. All these instruments – aiming at solving mostly sectorally defined structural and institutional weaknesses – must be used efficiently in combination with:

- effective and sustainable pro-growth and productivity-increasing policies, with attention to the terri- torial differentiation of development factors programmed and implemented by national and sub-national authorities; and
- more coordination at European level of globalisation and macroeconomic factors that are beyond the control of individual Member States and development partners.

At present, the ability of Member States and other development actors to implement ambitious pro- development policies is limited not only by the situation and development paths of the territories concerned but also by the way in which each globalisation and European integration process affects the social and economic lives of their citizens.

 https://doi.org/10.1080/2578711X.2019.1547491

7. CONCLUSIONS AND RECOMMENDATIONS

7.1 A NEW AGENDA FOR STRUCTURAL TRANSFORMATION AND COHESION

The EU model of integration has delivered long-term growth and economic and social convergence unmatched anywhere else in the world. However, the model is threatened by the uneven and unequal territorial and social effects of globalisation, technological change and EU integration on employment opportunities and living standards, combined with the difficulties or unwillingness of European societies to accept and integrate large-scale migration from poorer or war-torn parts of the world.

There is widespread public distrust in the ability of governments at national and EU levels to cope with these economic and social challenges. The EU and the process of EU integration have come under particular pressure, with political challenges to the legitimacy and accountability of the EU and its institutions. Brexit is the most prominent manifestation of this distrust, but it has been evident in almost every election and referendum held across the EU recent years, reflected in political polarisation and the rise of anti-EU parties or movements.

The challenge for the EU is not only to accelerate growth but also to resume convergence to ensure that all parts of the EU are able to exploit the growing globalisation of trade and technological change. In short, growth not only needs to be sustainable but also cohesive and inclusive, i.e. delivering prosperity across the whole of Europe.

Global transformations, especially technological change related to digitalisation and automation in the framework of transition towards the fourth production revolution, have significant implications, particularly with regard to jobs and off-shoring. They also represent an unprecedented opportunity, characterised by the OECD (with reference to the digitalisation of production) to be a major 'game changer' in reorienting global production and trade back towards developed countries.

Structural transformation should thus be at the heart of the renewal of EU policy priorities, as this will also determine the EU's capacity to cope and address other challenges. This means the empowerment of people, businesses and communities with the necessary skills, tools and institutions in order for them to excel in innovation as part of global value chains, but also to enable them to generate territorially distinct and differentiated products and services.

In order to do this, a new balance between policies for 'competitiveness' and 'cohesion' will need to be struck. As discussed in this book, the 'broken machine for diffusing technology means that aggregate productivity growth is faltering. The frontier continues to perform well, but regions that are diverging or keeping pace still represent 60 percent of EU GDP. Cohesion and competitiveness are therefore two aspects of the same objective – inclusive growth.

The effective promotion of inclusive growth requires the EU to reorganise its policy approach. It will need to facilitate a more coherent structural policy package that fully integrates the territorial dimension into the traditional frameworks of sectoral policies. The production of goods and services of the future requires well-functioning 'ecosystems' of open, interconnected networks of stakeholders, cooperating to a much greater extent through strategic partnerships, which will be much more dependent on their business

https://doi.org/10.1080/2578711X.2019.1547492

environments to source ideas and solutions both locally (e.g. importance of knowledge-based factors) and globally. Given that such ecosystems will often be regional/local, it is clear that EU sectoral policies alone cannot deliver inclusive growth.

The new structural transformation narrative requires a more territorially differentiated approach, backed by cross-sectoral coordination and alignment of policies across levels of government, which the economy-wide, space-blind approach was unable to achieve. This revised EU policy framework, which has to be more focused (on structural transformation), must put more emphasis on governance (bringing all relevant stakeholders on board) and realise that it can only deliver on EU objectives if it integrates policy instruments at different levels in a coherent policy approach: from the regulatory and structural reforms agenda to EU sectoral and integrated territorial policies. In so doing, the understanding of interrelationships will be critical for the inclusive growth agenda. Rural areas are dependent on cities, as are cities on rural areas. Well-performing metropolitan cities are not 'better' – their function and sectoral composition is simply different, and both types of area can gain from improved connectivity with each other.

7.2 RECOMMENDATIONS

1. The EU requires a new strategy for sustainable growth and structural transformation. This should set out a common policy vision for the territory of the EU for 10+ years ahead, with clear, achievable and manageable objectives. It needs to combine improved exploitation of the opportunities of globalisation through a more competitive and technologically advanced economy with the measures to ensure that this exploitation is sustainable, cohesive and inclusive i.e. that all countries and regions can take advantage of the opportunities. The strategy should provide a coherent framework for all EU policies – through regulatory reform, directly managed and territorial policies – with a collective focus on improving the ecosystems for structural change at EU, national, regional and other territorial levels when appropriate.

2. The ecosystems needed for structural change differ across countries, regions, cities and localities. Effective structural transformation therefore requires a commitment by governments at different levels to work together to facilitate concerted and integrated action, combining a mix of policy inputs, to meet different territorial development needs and challenges.

3. A reformed economic governance and coordination system for the whole EU (European Semester) should build an integrated framework for economic policy coordination, but ensure that it improves the conditions for structural transformation across all levels of government (EU, national, regional, local) and take account of territorial differences and diverse potentials within and between Member States. Future Country-Specific Recommendations should be multiannual and focus on the strategic reforms needed to achieve the new EU strategic goals for growth, structural transformation and cohesion.

4. Structural reforms require a mix of incentives and conditionalities to ensure that they are carried out. Any such mechanisms within the EU economic governance system should recognise that transformations are demanding processes requiring strategic and systematic efforts to be sustained over longer periods of time. Hence, incentives should be geared towards strategically designed investment and reforms for structural transformation at various territorial levels as opposed to simple ad hoc transfers and compensation schemes.

5. A new EU sustainable growth and structural transformation strategy should be underpinned by a performance and accountability framework covering all areas of EU spending, with a consistent and coherent approach to defining the rationale and logic of intervention, the contribution of objectives to the EU strategy, the anticipated outcomes, and the indicators and targets for assessing performance at national and sub-national levels.

    Structural transformation requires all levels of government to contribute to common EU objectives, ensuring their adaptation to regional and local development needs and challenges. This requires the empowerment of regional and local authorities and facilitating a more flexible and efficient dialogue with EU institutions, the business community and the public (citizens) to respond to globalisation and the opportunities and threats associated with the European integration process.

6. The 2013 reform of Cohesion Policy went a considerable way towards developing and implementing the essential components of the structural reform agenda. The reforms for 2021–2027 would ideally maintain the key principles of the 2013 regulatory changes (strategic coherence, thematic concentration – but without mandatory thematic objectives – performance focus, integrated territorial development) but involve specific changes to maximise opportunities to influence structural transformation, while addressing the remaining weaknesses of the policy. These changes include the following:
    a. alignment of objectives and priorities with the proposed new EU sustainable growth and structural transformation strategy in order to deliver inclusive growth;
    b. better coordination between competitiveness and cohesion agendas, including re-focusing and coordination between Cohesion Policy, other EU policies and national policies that have a major role in achieving the objectives of structural transformation defined at EU, national and sub-national levels;
    c. recognition at strategic level (EU sustainable growth and structural transformation strategy) and in implementation (various EU policies) of the different territorial opportunities and challenges for different types of regions (frontier, intermediate and lagging) to deliver the structural transformation agenda by differentiating support in the designation of regions, financial allocation of resources, and/or the design of strategies;[21]

---

[21] It should also be recognised that regional and national performances are linked and especially that the frontier regions of less-developed Member States play a key role in the structural transformation agendas of their respective countries.

https://doi.org/10.1080/2578711X.2019.1547492

d. a stronger commitment to human capital support, given the critical role of education and skills for structural transformation, focusing on building effective educational, employment and training systems in the Member States, and ensuring that EU-level human capital policy intervention is differentiated according to the varying development needs and challenges of different countries and regions and delivered in an integrated manner;

e. re-focusing conditionalities to incentivise Member States to create the programming, legal and institutional frameworks for implementing the structural transformation agenda, ensuring that funding is allocated in line with the set objectives and policies, and with the achievement of agreed conditions;

f. investment in building institutional capacity, especially leadership and human resources and a multilevel system of governance, capable of developing policies and implementing interventions for structural transformation and cohesion;

g. strategic programming of Cohesion and other EU policies at national level focused on implementing structural transformation at different territorial levels, linked directly with the economic governance coordination system;

h. a significantly rationalised implementation system based on the principles of rationalisation of programming, more flexibility for national implementation systems, differentiated management, simplified financial management and control, and a significant reduction of administration for all entities (implementing bodies and beneficiaries) involved in programme administration;

i. introduction of an EU-wide Technical Assistance programme for all levels of government to facilitate the structural transformation agenda and enhance cooperation networks between different tiers of government and their interactions with private and social partners.

Set against these principles, the proposals from the European Commission for the 2021–2027 period (European Commission 2018c) fall short of what is required. On the positive side, there is some recognition of the importance of structural growth transformation, reflected in the increased emphasis placed on research and innovation. 'Digital Europe' and SME competitiveness. Reforms have been introduced to economic governance, going at least partly in the direction of proposals in this book, and structural reforms are being incentivised together with conditionalities. The new Structural Reform Programmes and Service should boost support for national and regional governments to facilitate structural reforms. A significant degree of simplification is proposed. There are some interesting proposals to promote the diffusion of technology, though on a minor scale.

Where the Commission's proposals fail (and significantly so) is to set out an EU strategy for structural growth and transformation with a common vision for the EU as a whole. They do not provide a framework for improving the ecosystems for structural change in ways that integrate the efforts of different levels of government to address the different development opportunities and constraints of countries, regions, cities and localities. Sectoral policy thinking predominates over a territorial perspective. Notwithstanding the language and mechanisms to link Cohesion Policy with EU policies for research, innovation and investment, the proposals would see less coherence in the EU's policy response to cohesion, especially the relationship between the ERDF/Cohesion Fund with the ESF+ and, even more so, with EU policies for rural development. The principle of thematic concentration continues to be applied prescriptively (albeit at national rather than programme levels), and there must be concern at the insufficient emphasis placed on transformational activities, especially under the smart growth objective, at least for certain countries and regions. Further, the incentives for Member States to strengthen multilevel governance and the empowerment of subnational authorities remain too weak, despite the flexibility that has been introduced. Redressing the overly centralised approach to Cohesion Policy governance in a number of countries is not on the agenda. A performance and accountability framework covering all policies continues to be lacking.

In short, it is difficult to see how the proposals will narrow the gap between the frontier regions and lagging or catching up regions. Whether the Commission's proposals can be modified in the direction of a more effective 'Cohesion Policy 4.0' depends significantly on the Council and European Parliament.

Finally, it is important to emphasise that this book's advocacy of a comprehensive and integrated approach to inclusive growth rests on the legal provisions of the Treaty on the Functioning of the European Union, which states that the pursuit of economic, social and territorial cohesion is a collective task of both national and EU policies. Article 175 makes clear that Member States have the primary responsibility for the conduct and coordination of their economic policies to meet cohesion objectives. The same obligation applies to all EU policies and actions, including the implementation of the internal market.

The agenda for 'Cohesion 4.0' is therefore, a much wider task than for Cohesion Policy alone. It requires Member States to demonstrate that they have implemented structural reforms to support growth and cohesion before uploading domestic interests to the European level. It also underscores the necessity of an integrated approach to structural transformation and cohesion under all EU regulatory and investment policies.

8. BIBLIOGRAPHY

Ahrend R and Schumann A (2014) Does Regional Economic Growth Depend on Proximity to Urban Centres? *OECD Regional Development Working Papers, 2014/07*, OECD Publishing, Paris.

Aiginger K (2016) *New Dynamics for Europe. Reaping the Benefits of a Socio-Ecological Transition. Part I: Synthesis – Executive Summary, WWWforEurope Synthesis Report*, Vienna/Brussels: European Commission.

Alecke B, Blien U, Frieg I, Otto A and Untiedt G (2010) *Ex post evaluation of Cohesion Policy programmes 2000–2006 financed by the ERDF: Enterprise Support – an exploratory study using counterfactual methods on available data from Germany*, Final report to the European Commission (DG Regional Policy), GERFRA, Münster and IAB: Nürnberg.

Altus (2016) *The use of new provisions during the programming phase of the European Structural and Investment Funds*, Final Report to the Directorate-General for Regional and Urban Policy, European Commission, May 2016.

Amison P and Bailey D (2014) Phoenix industries and open innovation? The Midlands advanced automotive manufacturing and engineering industry, *Cambridge Journal of Regions, Economy and Society*, 7(3), 397–412.

Andrews D, Criscuolo C and Gal P N (2016) *The Best versus the Rest: The Global Productivity Slowdown, Divergence across Firms and the Role of Public Policy*, OECD Productivity Working Papers, 2016-05, OECD Publishing, Paris.

Arntz M, Gregory T and Zierahn U (2016) The risk of automation for jobs in OECD countries: a comparative analysis, *OECD Social, Employment and Migration Working Papers*, No 189. Paris: OECD Publishing, Paris.

Autor D, Dorn D and Hanson G (2013) The China syndrome: Local labour market effects of import competition in the United States, *American Economic Review*, 103(6), 2121–2168.

Autor D H (2015) Why Are There Still So Many Jobs? The History and Future of Workplace Automation, *Journal of Economic Perspectives*, 29(3), 3–30.

Bachtler J, Begg I, Polverari L and Charles D (2016) *EU Cohesion Policy in Practice: What Does It Achieve?* Rowman & Littlefield International.

Bachtler J and Begg I (2018) Beyond Brexit: Reshaping policies for regional development in Europe, *Papers in Regional Science*, 97(1), 151–170.

Bachtler J and Mendez C (2016) *Differentiation in the management of Cohesion policy: an idea whose time has come?* http://tinyurl.com/hozwf9k.

Bachtler J and Polverari L, with McMaster I and Lehuraux T (2017) *Building Blocks for a Future Cohesion Policy – First Reflections*, Research for the REGI Committee, DG for Internal Policies, European Parliament, Brussels.

Badinger H, Bailey D, De Propris L, Huber P, Janger J, Kratena K, Pitlik H, Sauer T, Thillaye R and van den Bergh J (2016) *New Dynamics for Europe: Reaping the Benefits of Socio-ecological Transition. Part II: Model and Area Chapters*, WWWforEurope Synthesis Report, Vienna/Brussels: European Commission.

Bailey D and De Propris L (2002) The 1988 Reform of the Structural Funds: Entitlement or Empowerment? *Journal of European Public Policy*, 9(3).

https://doi.org/10.1080/2578711X.2019.1547493

Bailey D and De Propris L (2014) Manufacturing Reshoring and its Limits: the UK Automotive Case, *Cambridge Journal of Regions, Economy and Society*, 7(3), 379–398.

Balcerzak A P (2015) Europe 2020 Strategy and Structural Diversity Between Old and New Member States. Application of Zero Unitarization Method for Dynamic Analysis in the Years 2004–2013, *Economics and Sociology*, 8(2), 190–210.

Balsvik R, Jensen S and Salvanes K G (2013) Made in China, sold in Norway: Local labour market effects of an import shock, *Journal of Public Economics*, 127, 137–144.

Barca F (2009) *An agenda for a reformed cohesion policy: A place-based approach to meeting European Union challenges and expectation*, Independent Report to the Commissioner of Regional and Urban Policy, Brussels.

Beaudonnet L and Gomez R (2016) Red Europe versus no Europe? The impact of attitudes towards the EU and the economic crisis on radical-left voting, *West European Politics*, 40:2, 316–335.

Becker S O, Egger P H and Von Ehrlich M (2010) Going NUTS: The Effect of EU Structural Funds on Regional Performance, *Journal of Public Economics*, 94(9–10), 578–590.

Begg I (2016) 'The Economic Theory of Cohesion Policy' in Piattoni S and Polverari L (eds) *Handbook on Cohesion Policy in the EU*, Edward Elgar.

Bell B and Machin S (2016) *Brexit and Wage Inequality*, Centre for Economic Performance, London School of Economics: London.

Beugelsdijk M and Eijffinger S (2005) The effectiveness of structural policy in the European Union: An empirical analysis for the EU-15 in 1995–2001, *Journal of Common Market Studies* 40, 37–51.

Boldrin M and Canova F (2001) Inequality and convergence in Europe's regions: reconsidering European regional policies, *Economic Policy*, 16(32), 205–253.

Bondonio D and Martini A (2012) *Counterfactual impact evaluation of Cohesion policy: Impact and cost-effectiveness of investment subsidies in Italy*, Final report to the European Commission (DG Regional Policy), Torino.

Bondonio D and Pellegrini G (2016) *Ex post evaluation of Cohesion Policy programmes 2007–2013, focusing on the European Regional Development Fund (ERDF) and the Cohesion Fund (CF): Macro-economic effects of Cohesion policy funding in 2007–2013, Work Package 14c: Regression discontinuity design and Work Package 14d: Propensity score matching: Executive Summary*, Report to the European Commission DG for Regional and Urban Policy.

Börzel T and Risse T (2017) From the euro to the Schengen crisis: European integration theories, politicization, and identity politics, *Journal of European Public Policy*. doi: 10.1080/13501763.2017.1310281.

Boston Consulting Group (2014) *The Shifting Economics of Global Manufacturing*. The Boston Consulting Group, Boston.

Bradley J and Untiedt G (2009) *Analysis of EU Cohesion policy 2000–2006 using the CSHM: aggregate impacts and inter-country comparisons*, Final Report to the European Commission (DG Regional Policy): Dublin.

Brakman S and van Marrewijk C (2007). *It's a Big World After All*. CESifo Working Paper No. 1964, 41.

Brandsma A, Kancs d'A, Monfort P and Rillaers A (2013) *RHOMOLO: a dynamic spatial general equilibrium model for assessing the impact of Cohesion policy*, Working paper of the European Commission (DG Regional Policy) No.1/2013: Brussels.

Breemersch K, Damijan J P and Konings J (2016) *Labor Market Polarization in Advanced Countries: Impact of Global Value Chains, Technology, Import Competition from China and Labor Market Institutions*, working paper prepared for the OECD.

Breidenbach P, Mitze T and Schmidt C M (2016) EU Structural Funds and Regional Income Convergence – A sobering experience, *Ruhr Economic Papers* #608.

https://doi.org/10.1080/2578711X.2019.1547493

Buti M and Pichelman K (2017) *European integration and populism: addressing Dahrendorf's quandary*, Policy brief, LUISS School of European Political Economy.

Chalmers A W and Dellmuth L M (2015) Fiscal redistribution and public support for European integration. *European Union Politics*, 16(3), 386–407.

Charron N, Dijkstra L and Lapuente V (2014) Regional governance matters: Quality of government within European Union member states. *Regional Studies*, 48(1), 68–90.

Charron N, Dijkstra L and Lapuente V (2015) Mapping the Regional Divide in Europe: A Measure for Assessing Quality of Government in 206 European Regions, *Social Indicators Research*, 122(2), 315–346.

Chesbrough H W (2003) The Era of Open Innovation, *MIT Sloan Management Review*, 44(3), 35–41.

Cheshire P and Magrini S (2000) Endogenous Process in European Regional Growth: Convergence and Policy, *Growth and Change*, 31(Fall), 455–479.

Chui M, Manyika J and Miremadi M (2015) Four fundamentals of workplace automation, *McKinsey Quarterly*, November 2015.

Cincera M and Veugelers R (2014) Differences in the rates of return to R&D for European and US young leading R&D firms, *Research Policy* 43(8), 1413–1421.

Clarke H D, Goodwin M and Whiteley P (2017) *Brexit: Why Britain voted to leave the EU*, Cambridge: Cambridge University Press.

Coe N and Yeung H (2015) *Global Production Networks*, Oxford: Oxford University Press.

Colliers International and Corenet Global (2013) *Home vs. Away, The Repatriation of Manufacturing in Europe, Report*. London: Colliers.

Comin AvD and Mestieri Ferrer M (2013) *If Technology Has Arrived Everywhere, Why Has Income Diverged*, NBER Working Paper Series, May.

Council of the European Union (2014) *Europe 2020 strategy mid-term review – Synthesis report*, Brussels, 15 December 2014 (OR. en) 16559/14.

Crescenzi R, Luca D and Milio S (2016a) The geography of the economic crisis in Europe: national macroeconomic conditions, regional structural factors and short-term economic performance, *Regions, Economy and Society*, 9(1), 13–32.

Crescenzi R, Fratesi U and Monastiriotis V (2016b) 'The achievements of cohesion policy: long period evidence on the factors conditioning success and failure from 15 selected regions', in Dotti N. (ed.) *Learning from Implementation and Evaluation of Cohesion Policy – Lessons from a Research-Policy Dialogue*, published by the Regional Studies Association (RSA) Research Network on Cohesion Policy.

Criscuolo C, Martin R, Overman H and Van Reenen J (2012) *The causal effects of an industrial policy*, Centre for Economic Performance (CEP) Discussion Paper No 1113: London School of Economics and Political Science, London.

CSIL, Joanneum Research, Technopolis Group, in association with Nordregio and KITE (2010) *Contract No. 2008. CE.16.0.AT.020 concerning the ex post evaluation of cohesion policy programmes 2000–2006 co-financed by the European Regional Development Fund (Objectives 1 and 2), Work Package 4 'Structural Change and Globalisation'*, Final Report to the European Commission, Directorate-General for Regional and Urban Policy, Centre for Local and Industrial Strategies, Milan.

Dall'erba S and Le Gallo J (2008) Regional convergence and the impact of European structural funds over 1989–1999: A spatial econometric analysis, *Regional Science*, 87(2), 219–244.

Daly M (2012) Paradigms in EU social policy: a critical account of Europe 2020, *Transfer: European Review of Labour and Research*, 18(3) 273–284.

Darvas Z and Wolff G B (2016) *An Anatomy of Inclusive Growth in Europe*, Blueprint Series 26, Bruegel: Brussels.

Dauth W, Findeisen S and Suedekum J (2014) The rise of the East and the Far East: German labor markets and trade integration, *Journal of the European Economic Association*, 12(6), 1643–1675.

Davies S (2015) Is simplification simply a fiction? *IQ-Net Thematic Paper* 37(2), European Policies Research Centre, University of Strathclyde, Glasgow.

Davies S (2017) *Meta-Review of Research on the Effectiveness of Cohesion Policy*, European Policy Research Papers, Number 99, European Policies Research Centre, University of Strathclyde, Glasgow.

De Backer K, Menon C, Desnoyers-James I and Moussiegt L (2016) *Reshoring: Myth or Reality?* OECD Science, Technology and Industry Policy Papers, No. 27, OECD Publishing, Paris. DOI: http://dx.doi.org/10.1787/5jm56fr bm38s-en.

D'Costa S, Garcilazo E and Oliveira Martins J (2018) Impact of Structural Reforms on the Productivity of Regions, *Papers in Regional Science*, 1–34.

Delmas A (2015) *Perspectives for revision of the Europe 2020 strategy*, Opinions of the Economic Social and Environmental Council, Economic Social and Environmental Council of the French Republic, June 2015, http://www.eesc.europa.eu/resources/docs/strategieeurope2020.pdf.

De Propris L / World Economic Forum (2016) *How the Fourth Industrial revolution is powering the rise of Smart Manufacturing.* https://www.weforum.org/agenda/2016/06/how-the-fourth-industrial-revolution-is-powering-the-rise-of-smart-manufacturing.

De Vries C and Hoffman I (2016) *Globalisierungsangst order Wertekonflikt: Wer in Europa populistische Parteien wählt und warum,* eupinions, Bertelsmann Stiftung.

Dicken P (2014) *Global Shift. Mapping the Changing Contours of the World Economy*, London: Sage.

Dijkstra L and Athanasoglou S (2015) The Europe 2020 Index. The Progress of EU Countries, Regions and Cities to the 2020 Targets, *Regional Focus*, 01/2015, May 2015.

Directorate-General for Employment and Social Affairs (2015) *Performance Monitoring Report of the European Union Programme for Employment and Social Innovation (EaSI) 2014*. Brussels: European Commission.

Donoso V, Martin V and Minondo A (2014) Do differences in the exposure to Chinese imports lead to differences in local labour market outcomes? An analysis for Spanish provinces. *Regional Studies*, 34(4), 1–19.

Duranton G and Overman G H (2005) Testing for Localization Using Micro-Geographic Data, *The Review of Economic Studies*, 72(4), 1077–1106.

Ederveen S, Groot H L F and Nahuis R (2006) Fertile soil for structural funds? A panel data analysis of the conditional effectiveness of European cohesion policy, *Kyklos*, 59(1), 17–42.

Ellram L, Tate W and Petersen K (2013) Offshoring and Reshoring: An Update On The Manufacturing Location Decision, *Journal of Supply Chain Management*, 49(3), 14–22.

Ernst and Young (2016) *Ad-hoc audit of the application of the Regulation 2015/1017 (the EFSI Regulation).* Final report prepared for the European Commission. Available at: https://ec.europa.eu/commission/sites/beta-political/files/ey-report-on-efsi_en.pdf.

Esposti R and Bussoletti S (2008) Impact of Objective 1 funds on regional growth convergence in the European Union: A panel-data approach, *Regional Studies* 42(2), 159–173.

European Commission (2005a) *Public Opinion in the European Union*, Standard Eurobarometer 62, May 2005, Commission of the European Communities, Brussels.

European Commission (2005b) *Working together for growth and jobs, a new start for the Lisbon strategy Communication to the Spring European Council*, Communication from President Barroso in agreement with Vice-President Verheugen, SEC(2005)192, SEC(2005)193, COM(2005) 24 final.

https://doi.org/10.1080/2578711X.2019.1547493

European Commission (2010a) *Lisbon Strategy evaluation document,* Commission staff working document, Brussels, 2.2.2010, SEC(2010)114 final, 2 February 2010, Brussels.

European Commission (2014a) *Investment for jobs and growth; Promoting development and good governance in EU regions and cities,* Sixth report on economic, social and territorial cohesion, Brussels.

European Commission (2014b) *Taking stock of the Europe 2020 strategy for smart, sustainable and inclusive growth,* Communication from the Commission to the European Parliament, the Council, the European Economic and Social Committee and the Committee of the regions., COM(2014) 130 final/2, 19 March 2014, Brussels.

European Commission (2015b) *Examples of EU added value. Accompanying document.* Commission Staff Working Document, Report from the Commission to the European Parliament and the Council on the evaluation of the Union's finances based on the results achieved {COM(2015) 313 final} {SWD(2015) 125 final}, Brussels, 26.6.2015 SWD (2015) 124 final, http://ec.europa.eu/smart-regulation/evaluation/docs/swd1_2014_en.pdf.

European Commission (2015c) *Results of the public consultation on the Europe 2020 strategy for smart, sustainable and inclusive growth,* Communication from the Commission to the European Parliament, the Council, the European and Social Committee and the Committee of the Regions. COM(2015) 100 final, 2 March 2015, Brussels.

European Commission (2016a) *Public opinion in the European Union,* Standard Eurobarometer 86, Autumn 2016, Commission of the European Communities, Brussels.

European Commission (2016b) *Regional Innovation Scoreboard 2016,* Brussels.

European Commission (2016c) *European Economic Forecast,* Institutional Paper 38, Statistical Annex, Publications Office of the European Union, Luxembourg.

European Commission (2016d) *Future of Europe,* Special Eurobarometer 451, Commission of the European Communities, Brussels.

European Commission (2016e) *Mid-term review/revision of the multiannual financial framework 2014-2020. An EU budget focused on results.* Commission Staff Working Document Accompanying the Document – Communication from the Commission to the European Parliament and the Council – Brussels: SWD(2016) 299 final.

European Commission (2016f) *Mid-term review/revision of the multiannual financial framework 2014–2020. An EU budget focused on results,* Communication from the Commission to the European Parliament and the Council, COM(2016) 603 final, Brussels.

European Commission (2016g) *Horizon 2020 Monitoring Report 2015,* DG Research, Brussels.

European Commission (2017a) *Competitiveness in low-income and low-growth regions. The lagging regions report,* Commission Staff Working Document, SWD(2017) 132 final, 10 April 2017, Brussels.

European Commission (2017b) *Reflection Paper on Harnessing Globalisation,* COM (2017) 240, Brussels.

European Commission (2017c) *Reflection paper on the Social Dimension of Europe,* 26 April 2017, Brussels.

European Commission (2017d) *The Value Added of Ex ante Conditionalities in the European Structural and Investment Funds,* Commission Staff Working Document, SWD(2017)127, Brussels.

European Commission (2017e) *Seventh Report on Economic, Social and Territorial Cohesion,* Brussels.

European Commission (2018a) *Public opinion in the European Union,* Standard Eurobarometer 89, Summer 2018, Commission of the European Communities, Brussels.

European Commission (2018b) *European Economic Forecast,* Institutional Paper 77, Statistical Annex, Publications Office of the European Union, Luxembourg.

European Commission (2018c) *A Modern Budget for a Union that Protects, Empowers and Defends – the Multiannual Financial Framework for 2021–2027,* COM(2018) 321 final, 2 May 2018, Brussels.

European Council (2000) Presidency Conclusions, 23–24 March 2000, Brussels.

European Court of Auditors (2016) FSI: an early proposal to extend and expand, Opinion No 2/2016 (pursuant to Article 287(4) of the Treaty on the Functioning of the European Union (TFEU)) concerning the proposal for a Regulation of the European Parliament and of the Council amending Regulations (EU) Nos 1316/2013 and 2015/1017 and the accompanying Commission evaluation in accordance with Article 18(2) of Regulation (EU) 2015/1017, Luxembourg.

European Court of Auditors (2017) *The Commission's negotiation of 2014–2020 Partnership Agreements and programmes in Cohesion: spending more targeted on Europe 2020 priorities, but increasingly complex arrangements to measure performance*, Special Report No. 2/2017, Luxembourg.

European Court of Auditors (2017) *Selection and monitoring for ERDF and ESF projects in the 2014-2020 period are still mainly outputs-oriented*, Special report no 21/2018, Luxembourg.

European Investment Bank (EIB) (2016) *Operations Evaluation – Evaluation of the functioning of the European Fund for Strategic Investments (EFSI)*. Report carried out by the EIB's Operations Evaluation Division, Luxembourg.

Faiña A J, López-Rodríguez J and Montes-Solla P (2016) Cohesion policy and transportation, in Piattoni S and Polverari L (eds) *Handbook on Cohesion policy in the EU*, Edward Elgar: Cheltenham, 339–358.

Farole T, Rodríguez-Pose A and Storper M (2011) Cohesion Policy in the European Union: Growth, Geography, Institutions. *Journal of Common Market Studies*, 49, 1089–111.

Feldman M P and Kogler D (2010) Stylized facts in the geography of innovation, in Hall B H and Rosenberg N (eds) *Economics of Innovation*, Elsevier: Amsterdam, 411–427.

Ferrara A R, McCann P, Pellegrini G, Stelder D and Terribile F (2017) Assessing the impacts of Cohesion Policy on EU regions: a non-parametric analysis on interventions promoting research and innovation and transport accessibility, *Papers in Regional Science*, DOI: 10.1111/pirs.12234.

Ferry M, Kah S and Bachtler J (2016) *Maximisation of Synergies between European Structural Funds and Investment Funds and Other EU Instruments to Attain Europe 2020 goals,* IP/B/REGI/IC/2015-131, Report to the Committee on Regional Development (European Parliament, European Policies Research Centre, University of Strathclyde, Glasgow.

Francesca F and Sylvain G (2010) *Breaking out of policy silos: doing more with less*, Local Employment and Economic Development Organisation for Economic Cooperation and Development, Paris.

Frey C B and Osborne M A (2013) *The Future of Employment: How Susceptible are Jobs to computerisation?* Oxford Martin School Working Paper, Oxford University: Oxford.

Fujita M, Krugman P and Venables A (1999) *The Spatial Economy: Cities, Regions, and International Trad*. MIT Press, Cambridge, Mass.

Furik A (2016) EFSI boss: the next budget will be different, *EURACTIV*, 2 November 2016.

Gereffi G and Fernandes-Stark K (2011) *Global Value Chain Analysis: A Primer,* Center on Globalization, Governance & Competitiveness, Duke University, Durham, North Carolina, USA.

Goodwin M and Heath O (2016) *Brexit vote explained: poverty, low skills and lack of opportunities*, Joseph Rowntree Trust.

Goos M, Konings J and Vanderweyer M (2015) *Employment Growth in Europe: The Roles of Innovation, Local Job Multipliers and institutions*, Utrecht School of Economics Discussion Paper Series, Vol 15, No. 10.

Gray J V, Skowronski K, Esenduran G and Rungtusanatham M J (2013) The Reshoring Phenomenon: What Supply Chain Academics Ought To Know And Should Do, *Journal of Supply Chain Management*, 49(3), 27–33.

Gutiérrez J, Condeço-Melhorado A, López E and Monzón A (2011) Evaluating the European added value of TEN-T projects: a methodological proposal based on spatial spillovers, accessibility and GIS, *Journal of Transport Geography* 19, 840–850.

Hagen T and Mohl P (2008) Which is the right dose of EU Cohesion Policy for economic growth? *ZEW Discussion Paper No.* 08-104, Zentrum für Europäische Wirtschaftsforschung, Mannheim.

Haase D (2015) *The Cohesion Policy Dimension of the Implementation of the Europe 2020 Strategy. Study*, European Parliament, REGI Committee. http://www.europarl.europa.eu/RegData/etudes/STUD/2015/540361/IPOL_STU(2015)540361_EN.pdf

Hart M and Bonner K (2011) *Data-Linking and Impact Evaluation in Northern Ireland*, Final report to the European Commission (DG Regional Policy): Birmingham.

Henjak A, Tóka G and Sanders D (2012) Support for European Integration in Sanders D, Magalhaes P C and Tóka G (eds) *Citizens and the European Polity: Mass attitudes and National Polities*, Oxford University Press, Oxford.

High-Level Expert Group (2015) *Commitment and Coherence. Essential ingredients for success in science and innovation. Ex-post evaluation of the 7th EU framework programme (2007-2013)*. Brussels: High Level Expert Group.: https://www.ffg.at/sites/default/files/downloads/page/fp7_final_evaluation_expert_group_report.pdf

Hobolt S B and de Vries C (2016) Turning against the Union? The impact of the crisis on the Eurosceptic vote in the 2014 European Parliament elections, *Electoral Studies* 44, 504–14. doi: 10.1016/j.electstud.2016.05.006.

Hobolt S B and Tilley J (2016) Fleeing the centre: the rise of challenger parties in the aftermath of the Euro crisis, *West European Politics* 39(5), 971–991. doi: 10.1080/01402382.2016.1181871.

Hooghe L and Marks G (2004) Does identity or economic rationality drive public opinion on European integration? *Political Science and Politics*, 37(3), 415–420.

Hooghe L and Marks G (2017) Cleavage theory meets Europe's crises: Lipset, Rokkan, and the transnational cleavage, *Journal of European Public Policy* DOI: 10.1080/13501763.2017.1310279.

Iammarino S, Rodríguez-Pose and Storper M (2017) Why Regional Development Matters for Europe's Future, *DG Regio Working Paper* 7/2017, DG Regio, European Commission, Brussels.

International Monetary Fund (IMF) (2011) *Changing Patterns of Global Trade*, IMF Departmental Paper No. 12/1, Washington D.C.

Jorgenson Dale W, Ho M S and Samuels J D (2014) *US economic growth – retrospect and prospect: lessons from a prototype industry-level production account for the US, 1947–2012*, Cambridge University Press, Cambridge.

Ketels C and Protsiv S (2016) *European Cluster Panorama 2016*, European Cluster Observatory.

Keller W and Utar H (2016) *International trade and job polarization: Evidence at the worker-level. Technical Report 22315*, National Bureau of Economic Research.

Kharas H (2010) *The Emerging Middle Class in Developing Countries*, OECD Development Centre Working Papers, No. 285, OECD Publishing.

Kok W (2004) *Facing the challenge. The Lisbon strategy for growth and employment*, Report from the High Level Group chaired by Wim Kok, November 2004, Office for Official Publications of the European Communities, Luxembourg.

Kroll H, Copani G, Van de Velde E, Simons M, Horvat D, Jäger A, Wastyn A, PourAbdollahian G and Naumanen M (2016) *An analysis of drivers, barriers and readiness factors of EU companies for adopting advanced manufacturing products and technologies*, Report commissioned by DG Internal Market, Industry, Entrepreneurship and SMEs and prepared by Fraunhofer, VTT, IDEA and ITIA, European Commission, Brussels.

Krugman P (1994) *The Age of Diminishing Expectations*. MIT Press, Cambridge, Mass.

Kyriakou D (2017) *Smart Specialisation Concepts and Significance of Early Positive Signals*, European Structural and Investment Funds Journal, EStIF, 5(1), 4–11.

Kyriakou D, Palazuelos Martínez M, Períañez-Forte I and Rainoldi A (eds) (2017) *Governing Smart Specialisation*, Abingdon: Routledge.

Lastra-Anadón C and Muñiz M A (2017) Technological Change, Inequality and the Collapse of the Liberal Order, *Economics Discussion Papers, No.* 2017-43, Kiel Institute for the World Economy.

Los B, McCann P, Springford J and Thissen M (2017). The mismatch between local voting and the local economic consequences of Brexit, *Regional Studies* 51(5), 786–799.

Mabett D and Schekkle W (2007) Bringing Macroeconomics Back into the Political Economy of Reform: the Lisbon Agenda and the 'Fiscal Philosophy' of EMU, *Journal of Common Market Studies*, 45(1), 81–103.

Martin R, Sunley P, Tyler P and Gardiner B (2015) Divergent Cities in Post-Industrial Britain, *Structural Transformation, Adaptability and City Economic Evolutions Working Paper Number 1*. http://www.cityevolutions.org.uk/wp-content/uploads/Structural-Transformations-Working-Paper-1.pdf

Martin R, Sunley P, Gardiner B, Evenhuis E and Tyler P (2017) Structural Change and Productivity Growth in Cities, *Structural Transformation, Adaptability and City Economic Evolutions Working Paper Number 3*. http://www.cityevolutions.org.uk/wp-content/uploads/Structural-Dynamics-and-City-Growth-WP-3-2017-2.pdf

McCann P (2016) *The UK Regional-National Economic Problem: Geography, Globalisation and Governance*. London: Routledge.

McGregor A, Sutherland V, Tödtling-Schönhofer H and Naylon I (2014) *ESF Expert Evaluation Network Final synthesis report: Main ESF achievements, 2007–2013*. Report prepared for the Directorate General for Employment and Social Affairs, European Commission.

McKinsey & Company (2014) *Next-Shoring: A CEO's Guide, McKinsey Quarterly*, January 2014.

Mendez C and Bachtler J (2011) Administrative reform and unintended consequences: an assessment of the EU Cohesion policy 'audit explosion'. *Journal of European Public Policy*, 18(5), 746–765.

Mendez C, Kah S and Bachtler J (2011) Taking stock of programme progress: Implementation of the Lisbon Agenda and Lessons for Europe 2020, *IQ-Net Thematic Paper* 27(2), University of Strathclyde, European Policies Research Centre, Glasgow.

Mendez C and Bachtler J (2015) *Permanent revolution in Cohesion policy: restarting the reform debate*, EoRPA Paper 15/4, European Policies Research Centre, University of Strathclyde, Glasgow.

Mohl P and Hagen T (2010) Do EU structural funds promote regional growth? New evidence from various panel data approaches, *Regional Science and Urban Economics*, 40, 353–365.

Monfort P, Piculescu P, Rillaers A, Stryczynski K and Varga J (2016) *Ex post evaluation of Cohesion Policy programmes 2007–2013, focusing on the European Regional Development Fund (ERDF) and the Cohesion Fund (CF): Work Package 14a: The impact of cohesion policy 2007–2013: model simulations with Quest III*, European Commission DG Regional and Urban Policy.

Moretti E (2010) *Local Multipliers, American Economic Review*, Papers and Proceedings, No. 100, 1–7.

MT PRES (2017) *Presidency Paper: Cohesion Policy Post 2020: Bringing the Policy Closer to European Citizens*, Informal Meeting of Ministers responsible for Cohesion Policy, Valetta, 8–9 June 2017.

OECD (2010) *Breaking Out of Policy Silos: Doing More with Less, Local Economic and Employment Development (LEED)*, OECD Publishing. http://dx.doi.org/10.1787/9789264094987-en.

OECD (2011) *OECD Regional Outlook 2011: Building resilient regions for stronger economies*, OECD Publishing. http://dx.doi.org/10.1787/9789264120983-en.

OECD (2013a) *Interconnected Economies: Benefiting from Global Value Chains*, OECD Publishing.

OECD (2013b) *Challenges and Opportunities for Innovation through Technology: The Convergence of Technologies*, OECD Publishing.

OECD (2013c) *OECD Science, Technology and Industry Scoreboard 2013*, OECD Publishing. http://dx.doi.org/10.1787/sti_scoreboard-2013-en.

OECD (2014) *OECD Regional Outlook 2014: Regions and Cities: Where Policies and People Meet*, OECD Publishing. doi: 10.1787/9789264201415-en.

OECD (2015a) *ICTs and Jobs: Complements or Substitutes? The effects of ICT investment on Labour Market Demand by Skills and by industry in Selected Countries*, OECD Digital Economy Working Papers, No 259, OECD Publishing, Paris, http://dx.doi.org/10.1787/5jlwnklzplhg-en.

OECD (2015b) *ICTs, Jobs and Skills. New Evidence from the OECD PIAAC Survey*, internal document, OECD, Paris.

OECD (2015c) *Enabling the Next Production Revolution:* Issues Paper, background document prepared for the Danish Production Council conference 'Shaping the Strategy for Tomorrow's Production'.

OECD (2015d) *The Future of Productivity*, Working document prepared by the Economics Department, 27 February.

OECD (2015e) *The Future of Productivity*, OECD Publishing.

OECD (2016a) *Science, Technology and Innovation Outlook 2016: Megatrends affecting science, technology and innovation*, OECD Publishing.

OECD (2016b) *The Productivity-Inclusiveness Nexus*, document prepared for the Ministerial Council Meeting 2016. 4 May 2016.

OECD (2016c) *The Next Production Revolution – An Interim Project Report,* Document prepared by Directorate for Science, Technology and Innovation, 25 February.

OECD (2016e) *OECD Regional Outlook 2016: Productive Regions for Inclusive Societies*, OECD Publishing, Paris. http://dx.doi.org/10.1787/9789264260245-en.

OECD (2017a) *Key Issues for the Digital Transformation in the G20*; Report prepared for a joint G20 German Presidency / OECD conference, Berlin, Germany, 12 January 2017.

OECD (2017b) The Future of Global Value Chains: Business as usual or a new normal, Working document of Directorate for Science, Technology and Innovation, Paris, 27 March. (unpublished).

OECD (2017c) The Next Production Revolution: Implications for Governments and Business, OECD Publishing, Paris. http://dx.doi.org/10.1787/9789264271036-en.

OECD (2017d) *Economic Policy Reforms 2017: Going for Growth*, OECD Publishing, Paris. http://dx.doi.org/10.1787/growth-2017-en.

OECD (2018) *Productivity and Jobs in a Globalised World: (How) Can All Regions Benefit*? OECD Publishing, Paris.

Ogilvy and Mather (2016) *The Velocity 12 Report* http://www.campaignbriefasia.com/2016/06/17/V12%20Executive%20Summary.pdf

Ortega-Argilés R, Piva M and Vivarelli M (2015) The transatlantic productivity gap: Is R&D the main culprit?, *Canadian Journal of Economics*, 47(4), 1342–1371.

Oxman N (2016) *Age of Entanglement*, *Journal of Design and Science*, Featured On Jan 13.

Pelletier M (2017) RIS3 in the French Research and Innovation Context, *European Structural and Investment Funds Journal*, 5(1), 53–68.

Pilat D and Nolan A (2016) *Benefitting from the Next Production Revolution*, OECD Insights blog, Available at: http://wp.me/p2v6oD-2ph.

Polverari L, Bachtler J and Van der Zwet A (2014) Evaluating the Effectiveness of Regional Policy, *European Policies Research Paper* No. 91, European Policies Research Centre, University of Strathclyde, Glasgow.

Porter M E and Rivkin J W (2012) *The Looming Challenge to U.S. Competitiveness, Harvard Business Review*, March Issue.

PwC (2017) *Will robots steal our jobs? The potential impact of automation on the UK and other major economies*, Available at: https://www.pwc.co.uk/economic-services/ukeo/pwcukeo-section-4-automation-march-2017-v2.pdf.

Quah D (2011) The Global Economy's Shifting Centre of Gravity, *Global Policy*, 2(1), 3–9.

Ramboll Management Consulting (2015) *Ex-Post Evaluation of EURES covering the period 2009-2013*. Final Report prepared for DG Employment and Social Affairs of the European Commission. Available at: http://www.ec.europa.eu/social/BlobServlet?docId=15593&langId=en.

Rekers J V and Hansen T (2015) Interdisciplinary research and geography: Overcoming barriers through proximity, *Science and Public Policy* 42(2), 242–254.

Rifkin J (2014) *The Zero Marginal Cost Society: The internet of things, the collaborative commons, and the eclipse of capitalism*, New York: Palgrave Macmillan.

Rodríguez-Pose A (2013) Do institutions matter for regional development? *Regional Studies*, 47(7), 1034–1047.

Rodríguez-Pose A (2017) The revenge of the places that don't matter (and what to do about it). *Cambridge Journal of Regions, Economy and Society*, 11(1), 189–209.

Rodrik D (2009) Industrial policy: don't ask why, ask how, *Middle East Development Journal*, 2009, 1(1), 1–29.

Rodrik D (2013) Unconditional Convergence in Manufacturing, *Quarterly Journal of Economics*, 128(1), 165–204.

Roland Berger (2014) *Industry 4.0 – The new industrial revolution; How Europe will succeed*. Roland Berger Strategy Consultants.

Roland Berger (2015) *The digital transformation of industry,* Roland Berger Strategy Consultants. A European study commissioned by the Federation of German Industries.

Rooduijn M, Burgoon B, van Elsas E and van de Werfhorst H G (2017) Radical distinction: Support for radical left and radical right parties in Europe, *European Union Politics*, 18(4) 536–559,

Rosenthal S and Strange W (2003) *Geography, Industrial Organization, and Agglomeration, The Review of Economics and Statistics*, 85(2), 377–393.

Schäfer A (2012) Consequences of social inequality for democracy in Western Europe *Zeitschrift für vergleichende Politikwissenschaft*, 6, 23–45.

Schott P K (2008) *The Relative Sophistication of Chinese Exports, Economic Policy*, 53, 5–49.

Simpson K and Loveless M (2016) Another chance? Concerns about inequality, support for the European Union and further European integration. *Journal of European Public Policy*, 24(7), 1069–1089.

Smorodinskaya N, Russell M, Katukov D and Still K (2017) Innovation ecosystems vs. innovation systems in terms of collaboration and co-creation of value, Managing Platforms and Ecosystems Minitrack, http://hdl.handle.net/10125/41798

Smorodinskaya NV and Katukov D D (2017) Dispersed Model of Production and Smart Agenda of National Economic Strategies, *Economic Policy* Russian Presidential Academy of National Economy and Public Administration, vol. 6, pages 72–101, December.

Steer Davies Gleave (2011) *Mid-term evaluation of the TEN-T programme (2007–2013)*. Report prepared for the Directorate-General for Mobility and Transport of the European Commission. London: Steer Davies Gleave. https://ec.europa.eu/transport/sites/transport/files/facts-fundings/evaluations/doc/2011_ten_t.pdf.

Storper M and Venables A J (2004) Buzz: face-to-fact contact and the urban economy, *Journal of Economic Geography*, 4, 351–370.

Surubaru N C (2017) Administrative capacity or quality of political governance? EU Cohesion Policy in the new Europe, 2007–13, *Regional Studies*, 51(6), 844–856.

SYMOP, DGCIS, Gimelec, Roland Berger (2014) *Etude prospective a l'adaption de l'appareil productif francais*. Rapport final, May 2014. Paris.

Tilford S and Whyte P (2010) *The Lisbon scorecard X: The road to 2020*, Centre for European Reform, Available at: http://www.cer.org.uk/sites/default/files/publications/attachments/pdf/2011/rp_967-251.pdf.

https://doi.org/10.1080/2578711X.2019.1547493

Tomova M, Rezessy A, Lenkowski A and Maincent M (2013) EU governance and EU funds – testing the effectiveness of EU funds in a sound macroeconomic framework, *European Economy Economic Papers* No. 510.

Toth G and Nagy Z (2016) The world's economic centre of gravity, *Regional Statistics*, 6(2), 177–180.

Treib O (2014) The voter says no, but nobody listens: causes and consequences of the Eurosceptic vote in the 2014 European elections, *Journal of European Public Policy*, 21(10), 1541–1554.

Van der Zwet A, Bachtler J, Ferry M, McMaster I and Miller S (2017) *Strategies for integrated development: how are ESIF adding value in 2014–20?* Final Report to the European Commission (DG Regio), European Policies Research Centre, University of Strathclyde, Glasgow.

Van Rompuy H, Emmanouilidis J A and Zuleeg F (2017) Europe's reform opportunity, *Project Syndicate*, Avaialable at: https://www.project-syndicate.org/commentary/eurozone-reform-opportunity-by-herman-van-rompuy-et-al-2017-04.

Varga J and in t'Veld J (2010) The potential impact of EU Cohesion policy spending in the 2007-13 programming period a model-based analysis, *European Economy Economic Papers* No. 422.

Veneri P and Ruiz V (2013) *Urban-to-Rural Population Growth Linkages: Evidence from OECD TL3 Regions*, OECD Regional Development Working Papers, 2013/03, OECD Publishing, Paris. Available at: http://dx.doi.org/10.1787/5k49lcrq88g7-en.

Veugelers R (2015) Do we have the right kind of diversity in Innovation Policies among EU Member States? *WWWforEurope Working Paper Number 108*, Vienna/Brussels: European Commission.

Veugelers R and Cincera M (2010) Europe's Missing Yollies, *Bruegel Policy Briefs*, 06, Available at: http://ideas.repec.org/p/bre/polbrf/430.html.

Ward T, assisted by Greunz L, Fornoni R, Liberati F, Sanoussi F, Wolleb E, Naldini A, Ciffolilli A and Pompili M (2016) *Ex post evaluation of Cohesion Policy programmes 2007–2013, focusing on the European Regional Development Fund (ERDF) and the Cohesion Fund (CF): WP1: Synthesis report* by Applica and ISMERI Europa to the European Commission DG for Regional and Urban Policy.

Wostner P (2008) The Micro-efficiency of EU Cohesion Policy, *European Policy Research Papers, No. 64*. European Policies Research Centre, University of Strathclyde, Glasgow.

Wostner P (2017) *From Projects to Transformations: Why Do Only Some Countries and Regions Advance?* The Case of the Slovenian S4, *European Structural and Investment Funds Journal*, 5(1), 84–96.

Zgajewski T and Hajjar K (2005) *The Lisbon Strategy: Which failure? Whose failure? And why?*, Egmont Paper 6, Royal Institute for International Relations, http://aei.pitt.edu/8983/1/ep6.U701.pdf

ANNEX 1: REGIONAL PRODUCTIVITY CATCHING-UP IN SELECTED EU MEMBER STATES, 2000–2013

A. DISTRIBUTED PRODUCTIVITY MODEL

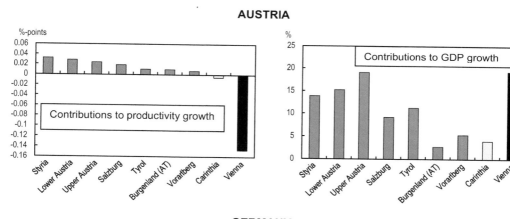

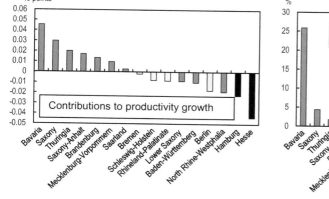

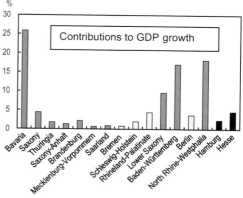

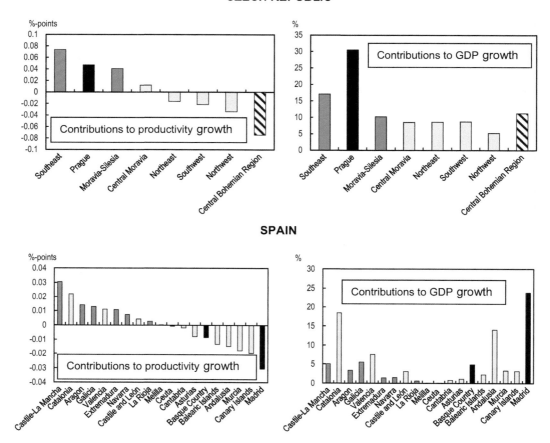

■ Frontier ▨ Catching up ☐ Keeping pace ▨ Diverging

CZECH REPUBLIC

SPAIN

ITALY

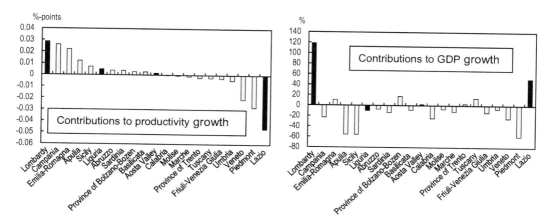

POLAND

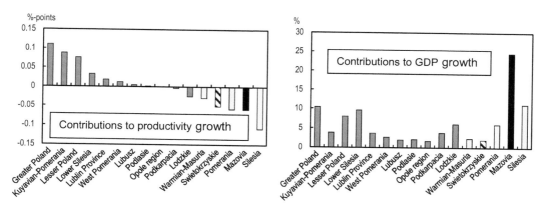

PORTUGAL

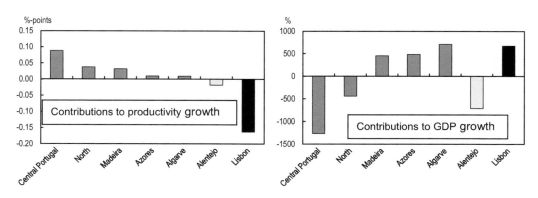

Note that the contribution to GDP growth in Portugal is complicated because of the very low or negative growth rates during the 2000–13 period.

ROMANIA

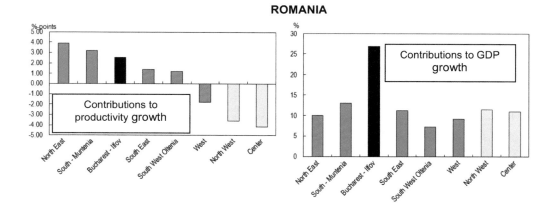

B. CONCENTRATED PRODUCTIVITY MODEL

■ Frontier ▦ Catching up ▢ Keeping pace ▨ Diverging

BULGARIA

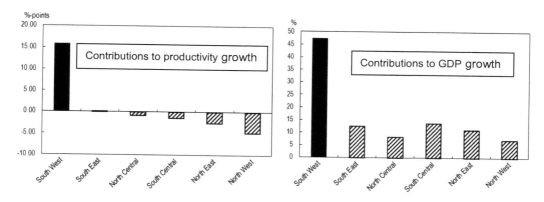

DENMARK

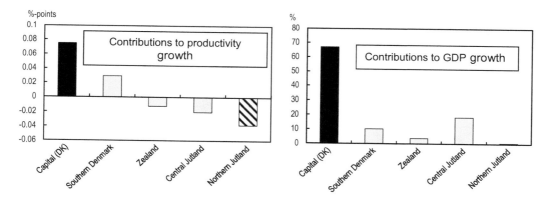

■ Frontier   ▨ Catching up   □ Keeping pace   ▨ Diverging

FRANCE

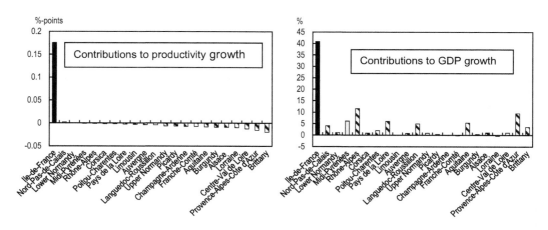

UNITED KINGDOM

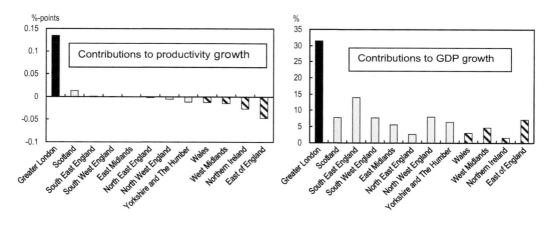

■ Frontier ▨ Catching up □ Keeping pace ▨ Diverging

GREECE

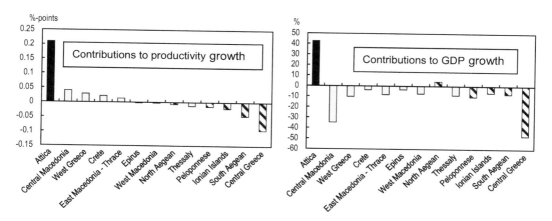

HUNGARY

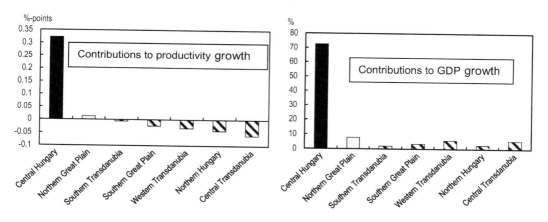

■ Frontier ■ Catching up □ Keeping pace ▨ Diverging

NETHERLANDS

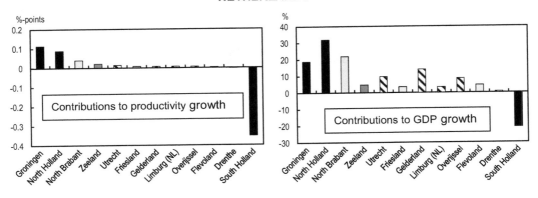

THE SLOVAK REPUBLIC

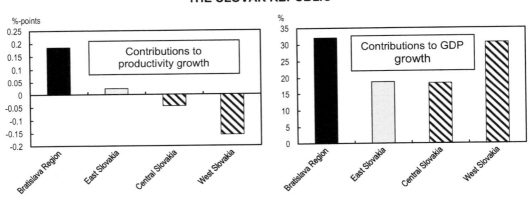

■ Frontier   ▨ Catching up   □ Keeping pace   ▨ Diverging

FINLAND

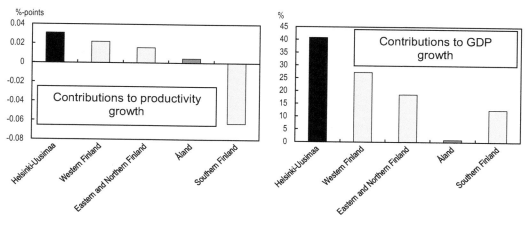

SWEDEN

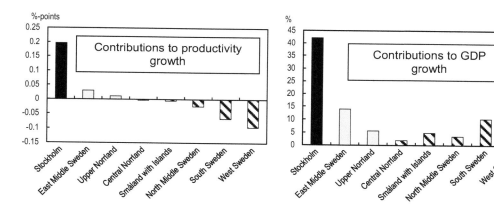

For Product Safety Concerns and Information please contact
our EU representative GPSR@taylorandfrancis.com Taylor & Francis
Verlag GmbH, Kaufingerstraße 24, 80331 München, Germany

T - #0295 - 160425 - C88 - 246/174/4 - PB - 9780367243678 - Matt Lamination